D1047257

Managing Management
Information Systems

Managing
Management
Information
Systems

T
58.6
.E33

Phillip Ein-Dor
Eli Segev
Tel-Aviv University

Lexington Books
D.C. Heath and Company
Lexington, Massachusetts
Toronto

INDIANA
UNIVERSITY LIBRARY

APR 17 1984

NORTHWEST

Library of Congress Cataloging in Publication Data

Ein-Dor, Phillip.
    Managing management information systems.

    Includes bibliographies.
    1. Management information systems. I. Segev, Eli., joint author.
II. Title.
T58.6.E33   658.4'5   77-10001
ISBN 0-669-01642-x

Copyright © 1978 by D.C. Heath and Company

All rights reserved. No part of this publication may be reproduced or transmit-
ted in any form or by any means, electronic or mechanical, including
photocopy, recording, or any information storage or retrieval system, without
permission in writing from the publisher.

Second printing, September 1979

Published simultaneously in Canada

Printed in the United States of America

International Standard Book Number: 0-669-01642-x

Library of Congress Catalog Card Number: 77-10001

Jwl   4-17-84

To our wives, Ita and Yael

Contents

List of Figures

List of Tables

Preface

The development of management information systems is an art, not a science. As with all arts, no simple, all-inclusive model explains the phenomena nor indicates the correct course of action. On the contrary, it is a very complex process, not yet well understood, that has many aspects which encompass a multitude of detail. One objective of this text is simply to organize this surfeit of detail coherently, by major issues, so that the reader may study the material systematically.

The literature on MIS is replete with articles addressing one or two of the numerous issues in the field, many of them pointing to one specific issue as being critically important. It is a basic tenet of this text that there is no single critical issue; on the contrary, each situation is unique and possesses its own set of critical points. This being the case, it is inappropriate to present recipes for MIS development and management. What is needed is a contingency plan, not a cookbook. Presenting the components for such a contingency plan is the second objective of this text.

As we point out the factors affecting the success and failure of MIS, we will present the different contingencies that may arise and methods of dealing with them. By the end of the book, we will have provided a checklist that can be applied to the analysis of any management information system situation. The actual application, however, is up to the reader. Applying the checklist to an individual situation will highlight its specific problems and in many cases will indicate the proper solution or perhaps its lack and consequent infeasibility of MIS development.

The book begins with an introductory chapter in which MIS concepts, definitions, and characteristics are presented and discussed. The text covers two main areas—procedural aspects of MIS and human aspects. The procedural aspects are covered in chapter 2, The MIS Environment; chapter 3, The MIS Target; and chapter 4, The MIS Project. Human aspects are dealt with in chapters 5 through 8, which cover executive responsibility, system implementors, MIS users, and intergroup relationships. Chapter 9, MIS Structure, deals with the interfaces between technological, organizational, and behavioral aspects of MIS and brings the text to a close in a section which contains our conclusions on the theory of MIS development.

Each chapter contains, in addition to the text and notes, a summary table that highlights its most significant points, as well as a list of suggested readings.

Our usage of the abbreviation MIS should be made clear. We use the same form both when we intend the singular management information system and for the plural management information systems. The plural form (MISs) seems to us to be particularly inelegant and we felt that we could rely on the intelligence of our readers to infer our intention from the syntactical context.

We are indebted to the Israel Institute of Business Research at Tel-Aviv University for its assistance in preparing this book and to Mrs. Tehilla Bletter whose critical and meticulous typing of the manuscript often spared us from our own errors and saved us many hours in proofing the manuscript. Finally, we hope the book justifies the encouragement, patience, and understanding of our families.

Tel-Aviv
September 1977

1 Introduction

Just as information systems are achieving recognition as one of the most powerful tools at the disposal of the modern manager, they are also becoming notorious as one of the most difficult tools. The thesis underlying this text is that the problems of information systems are caused primarily by improper or inadequate management. Exactly as the production, marketing, and finance functions of an organization need to be carefully managed, so does the information system function. This step requires the identification of problem areas and recommended solutions. Because management is still an art rather than a science, this book is devoted to the art of managing management information systems.

Many of the concepts we use in discussing information systems have not yet been rigorously or uniformly defined, including the concept of the management information system itself. Insofar as possible, we will do our best to rectify this situation. However, before we can get down to the details of managing MIS, we must first clarify some basic ideas. To ensure that we are all talking about the same things, we will first discuss *data* and *information* and their functions in the organization, then *management uses* of information in the organizational context, and finally *management information systems*.

MIS Concepts

Whenever we listen to speech or the sounds of nature, watch a television program, sniff the air, taste a morsel, or feel a texture we receive and process information. Similarly, when we talk, write, draw, or play music we are processing information and making it available to others. Thus information processing is one of the most pervasive, fundamental, and human of human activities. Some of our information-processing activities—such as painting, music, gastronomy, or theater-going—provide intellectual or sensual enjoyment. Other information-processing activities are much more pragmatic; for example, comparing prices, applying for jobs or scholarships, dodging the oncoming traffic, or being wary of hippogryphs.

Much of the information we need in our daily lives is not freely available but must be paid for either in cash or by our own exertions. Buying a newspaper, a book, or a ticket to a concert are obvious examples of

1

the first case. The costs are not always quite so obvious in the second case but are usually there. To avoid accidents I have to keep my eyes on the road when I would much rather watch the girls or the scenery. To collect information on items I am considering buying I may have to visit several stores, a costly process in terms of the time and energy consumed. Singing in the shower is one of the few examples of free information processing, but the information is not generally of much aesthetic or pragmatic value either.

Utility of Information

In the profit-oriented world of business, firms should be willing to incur the costs of processing information only if they can increase their profits or benefit in some other way that contributes to their well-being. Government and other nonprofit organizations should be interested in information that reduces their costs or increases their effectiveness. The question we must then ask is: "In what circumstances does information acquire value for an organization?" The answer requires that we first determine in what way information is useful to an organization.

Information for Operations and Management

Organizations use information in two main ways—in current operations and in management decision making. Information for current operations allows the organization to carry on its daily business. In a power company, for example, such information enables the company to send you a bill every month; it includes your name, address, tariff, and power consumption. In a supermarket, information about quantities of products on hand allows the store to know when to reorder. In a bank, the balances of the checking accounts provides it the information about which checks to honor and which to reject.

Unlike operational information, which is used daily and routinely, information for management is used as the need arises to enable the managers of the organization to control it or to make the decisions that change the organization or its business methods. For example, in the power company the decisions to build a new generating plant or to go from monthly billing to weekly billing are controlled by such information. In the supermarket, such decisions change the allocation of shelf space, introduce new products, or add check-out counters. In the bank, decisions of this type include extending additional credit to a customer, opening a new branch, offering a new service, or buying a new computer.

Many organizations tend to collect information that is not useful for either current operations or for management decision making—information for future reference or possible need. But if information is never used for operational or management decisions, it is of no value. Thus it is convenient to distinguish between information and data. Data are the original and detailed representations of events in the physical world. The number of kilowatts on Tom Smith's electric meter at the end of August is a datum. So is the inventory of one-pound cans of Calorifree brand chocolate fudge on hand at closing time on March 5. Every business, during its operations, generates vast amounts of data of this type. But because of their volume and level of detail, such items are useless, as they stand, for decision making; because of their lack of context, they are not even immediately applicable in current operations.

To turn Tom Smith's meter reading into a bill it must be considered in context—of his meter reading at the beginning of the month, the tariff table applicable to his account, and his delinquency record, as well as his address, of course. For such data to become useful in decision making, they will need to be condensed and processed. The total consumption of electricity in each month in the area served by the power company, compared to its generating capacity, might be one item considered in deciding whether to enlarge the plant. Thus data are the raw material from which information is manufactured by the operations known collectively as data processing. Those functions in the organization which process data are known variously as data processing systems, information systems, or, in special circumstances delineated later, management information systems.

We will now integrate our concepts of data and information with three models of organizations that are particularly pertinent to understanding the role of the information system in the organization. Two models, one developed by Robert Anthony, the other by Herbert Simon, relate to hierarchical aspects of organizations.

Hierarchy of Management Processes

Robert Anthony presents a hierarchical view of management processes consisting of three levels—strategic planning, management control, and operations control:[1]

Strategic planning is the process of deciding on objectives of the organization, on changes in these objectives, on the resources used to attain these objectives, and on the policies that are to govern the acquisition, use, and disposition of these resources.

Management control is the process by which managers assure that resources are obtained and used effectively and efficiently in the accomplishment of the organization's objectives.

Operational control is the process of assuring that specific tasks are carried out effectively and efficiently.

These processes tend to correspond to a consistent hierarchy along several dimensions. This conformity may be illustrated by table 1-1, adapted from Anthony's work.

To Anthony's three levels of management in organizations, we would add one more—the level of *operations*—the level of the lathe, the truck, the cash register, and the typewriter. At this level, the organization produces the goods and services it provides to the public and carries on its basic activities by which it tries to achieve its goals. The *operations* level is controlled by the *operations control* level of the hierarchy. With this addition, we obtain a four-level view of the organization as in figure 1-1.

Hierarchy in Decisions and Information

Herbert Simon defines management as being virtually synonymous with decision making.[2] The manager's job consists of recognizing circumstances that require decisions, identifying the appropriate action, and, finally, choosing the most effective action. But the amount of time spent making decisions varies considerably at the different hierarchical levels in an organization.

Simon distinguishes two levels of decision making and identifies the types of information and decision techniques employed at each level (see table 1-2).

Not only managers make decisions, however. Clerical and manual workers also have to make decisions, albeit somewhat trivial ones. For ex-

Table 1-1
Hierarchy of Management Processes

	Process		
Dimension	Strategic Planning	Management Control	Operations Control
Time span	long-range	medium-range	day-to-day
Level in organization	top management	top and operating management	supervision
Importance	major	medium	little
Amount of judgment	great	some	none

Source: Adapted from Robert N. Anthony. *Planning and Control Systems: A Framework for Analysis.* Boston: Division of Research, Graduate School of Business Administration, Harvard University (1965).

Figure 1-1. Hierarchy of Control Processes

ample, a machine operator has to decide when to start or stop his machine; a typist has to decide which paper to use and select a format and spacing. In Simon's model, such nonmanagerial decision making at the operational level appears under programmed decisions because workers typically follow standard procedures in making such choices.

Let us now superimpose Simon's hierarchy of programmed and unprogrammed decisions on our modified version of Anthony's model of control, as in figure 1-2. The two lowest levels of the control hierarchy, operations and operations control, correspond quite well to programmed decisions, and the top two levels of the control hierarchy correspond to unprogrammed decisions.

Drawing lines between the four levels of control and the two levels of programming only facilitates exposition. No such clear-cut boundaries exist in reality; there is, rather, a continuum of control processes that gradually change as one ascends the continuum in the hierarchy. The degree of programming in decision making also lessens the higher the level in the hierarchy. These two continua tend to change in parallel, and as the nature of control varies from operational to predominantly managerial to planning, so does the degree of programming in decisions decrease and the heuristic-intuitive content increase.

We can follow these parallel continua from the operational to the strategic levels and illuminate them by illustrations. First, the operations level of decision making and control is exemplified by the cashier in a bank deciding whether to honor a check. The cashier does not normally spend much time trying to recognize the need for a decision—it becomes obvious the moment the customer states his business. Nor does he have to agonize over appropriate courses of action; they are obvious and severely circumscribed. He can either pay the check or reject it. Finally, the particular action chosen is usually not left to the discretion of the cashier, but is dic-

Table 1-2
Traditional and Modern Techniques of Decision Making

Types of Decisions	Decision-Making Techniques	
	Traditional	Modern
Programmed Routine, repetitive decisions Organization develops specific processes for handling them	1. Habit 2. Clerical routine: Standard operating procedures 3. Organization structure: Common expectations A system of subgoals Well-defined information channels	1. Operations Research: Mathematical analysis Models Computer simulation 2. Electronic data processing
Nonprogrammed One-shot, ill-structured, novel policy decisions Handled by general problem-solving processes	1. Judgment, intuition, and creativity 2. Rules of thumb 3. Selection and training of executives	Heuristic problem-solving techniques applied to: a. training human decision makers b. constructing heuristic computer programs

Source: Herbert A. Simon. *The New Science of Management Decision*, rev. ed. Englewood Cliffs, N.J.: Prentice-Hall, 1977, p. 48. Reprinted with permission.

Figure 1-2. Hierarchy of Control and Decision Processes

tated by the manual of operations of the bank. The manual probably states that if the balance in the drawer's account is greater than or equal to the amount of the check, if the signature is valid, and if the date is within certain limits, the check is to be honored.

Thus at the level represented by the cashier, decision making is highly structured and circumscribed. Simon identifies this type of decision as *programmed decisions*, in the sense that a set of instructions, or program, unambiguously defines the actions to be taken in all conceivable circumstances. The information factored into this type of decision is either raw data (the check) or highly detailed information that has undergone only a minimum of processing (the balance in the drawer's account). This is what we called *operational information* in the preceding section.

The decision whether to honor a check is typical of a vast number of programmed decisions based on minimally processed data made at the lowest echelons of organizational hierarchies. Other examples include the decisions involved in payroll computation, in tax assessment, in reordering product X, in debiting account Y, or in billing customer Z. In fact, such activity is often programmed for computers, to which the decision making is then relegated. Decisions of this type are represented in figure 1-3, on the lowest level of the pyramid representing the organizational hierarchy.

The second level of the hierarchy is what Anthony calls "operational control." This level is characterized by decisions that are partly structured and circumscribed by established policy and partly unstructured, leaving certain issues to the discretion of the executive involved. For example, the quantities of products a shop foreman is to produce and the resources with which he is to produce them are dictated to him, but the particular worker assigned to each machine, the processes assigned to each worker, and the order in which items are produced are left to the foreman's judgment. The job of the branch manager in a bank is to control the operations of the

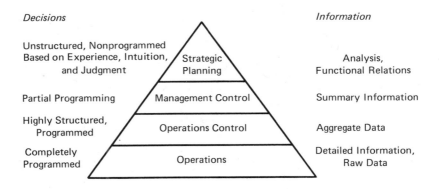

Decisions

Unstructured, Nonprogrammed
Based on Experience, Intuition,
and Judgment

Partial Programming

Highly Structured,
Programmed

Completely
Programmed

Strategic
Planning

Management Control

Operations Control

Operations

Information

Analysis,
Functional Relations

Summary Information

Aggregate Data

Detailed Information,
Raw Data

Figure 1-3. Hierarchical Structure: Organizational Control, Decisions, and Information

tellers and to ensure that they conform to the bank's procedures. He also has to make decisions in those cases which are referred to him because they are not completely covered by the rule book or contain some exceptional features not within the teller's sphere of competence—such as an overdrawn account of a very good customer.

The information required for making decisions at the operations control level is also somewhat different than that required at the lowest level. To continue the banking example, the teller needs only to know the balance in the customer's account; the branch manager, however, will want to know the customer's past record, how much business he does with the bank, and so forth. While still detailed and relating to a single customer, this information is more global and less specific. Furthermore, to manage his branch, the branch manager needs aggregate information on total deposits, number of customers, number of transactions, and total loans outstanding. At this level, although programming decisions is still possible, it becomes more difficult. Some additional processing and aggregation of data is also necessary.

The next level is that of managerial control or "middle management." Decisions at this level include, for example, approving routine capital investments, determining employment levels, locating branches and plants, and choosing operations managers. Company policy circumscribes the manager's activities, but leaves him considerable freedom within those bounds. At this level, the information required is available from detailed transactions only after a considerable amount of processing. Nor can the evaluation of such information be completely automatic, but a certain amount of experience and judgment are necessary to make it meaningful. This level of management is not passive and does not wait for problems to be brought to it, but tries to anticipate problems and solve them or at least prepare for them. Decisions at this level are not readily programmable and only the first steps have been taken in applying computers to them.

At the highest, strategic planning levels of management in the organization, not only are decisions completely unstructured and unprogrammed, but it is not always at all clear in which areas decisions need to be made. Top executives spend considerable time monitoring the environment and attempting to identify areas requiring attention. Is a new market developing that is related closely to the current product line? Has a new product been developed that might affect the market? Have new technologies been developed that might enable competition to undercut present costs? Is the economy developing in such a way that capital investments should be increased, or should expansion plans be cut back? Has the traditional bickering between sales and production reached a dangerous level? No manual of operations can guide the executive in choosing those questions which require answers. He must process large amounts of information, much of it originating from outside his organization. To this information he must apply his experience, intuition, and judgment in determining which problem areas are important enough to require his particular attention. The decision will frequently take the form of a policy statement that shapes decisions at the management control level.

Once the executive has determined, or circumstances have determined for him, on which areas he should focus, he must then devise a procedure for reaching a decision or formulating a policy. Problems at this level of management are usually sufficiently unique and nonrecurrent that the time and cost involved render it infeasible to establish fixed methods of solving them for several reasons. Because of the uniqueness of each problem, it is extremely difficult to establish routines for collecting and processing the necessary information. The information required tends to be complex, the result of a considerable amount of processing. Much of the information required does not originate in the firm itself but reflects situations and events in the firm's environment.

In conclusion, we find that top management spends much more time than lower echelons on identifying problems requiring attention. Isolating such problems and evaluating their solutions are highly unstructured activities and, therefore, not amenable to programming. The search for problems and solutions requires the production of complex information, which in turn is distilled from vast quantities of primitive data. Much of this information does not originate within the organization itself but must be obtained from external sources. The parallel between levels of management, decision techniques, and information are illustrated in figure 1-3.

In general, the higher the level in the organization the less programmed the decision process and the more highly processed the information required for making decisions.

Industrial Dynamics

Jay Forrester has formulated a third model containing important insights into the role of information in organizations.[3] It describes the state of the organization by information on the *levels* of various activities and entities in the organization. The number of employees, the rate of production, average sales, and raw materials inventory are all examples of the levels that together form a representation of the organization.

Activity in the organization takes the form of flows of physical values between the levels (see figure 1-4). Thus the production level receives a flow of employees from the employment level and a flow of raw materials from the raw material inventory level. The production level in turn releases a flow of finished goods to the appropriate inventory level.

In addition to physical values, each level produces information *representing* those values. This information flows into decision points that use it to regulate the rates of flow. These double flows of information and physical entities are shown in figure 1-5. As a result, a network of information flows are superimposed on the physical network and control it. According to Forrester:

An industrial organization is a complex, interlocking network of information channels. These channels emerge at various points to control physical processes such as hiring employees, building factories and producing goods.[4]

The composition and functioning of the decision points posited by Forrester are also of some interest. In the decision points, the apparent state of

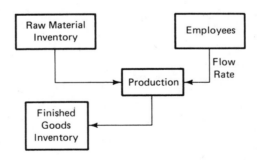

Source: Adapted from Jay W. Forrester, "Managerial Decision Making", in Martin Greenberger (ed). *Computers and the World of the Future* (1962), by permission of the M.I.T. Press, Cambridge, Massachusetts.

Figure 1-4. Flows and Levels Descriptions of Organizations

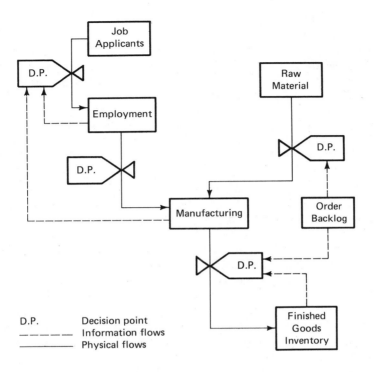

Job
Applicants

Raw
Material

D.P.

D.P.

Employment

D.P.

D.P.

Manufacturing

Order
Backlog

D.P.

Finished
Goods
Inventory

D.P.   Decision point
— — — —   Information flows
——————   Physical flows

Source: Adapted from Jay W. Forrester, "Managerial Decision Making", in Martin Greenberger (ed.) *Computers and the World of the Future* (1962), by permission of the M.I.T.
Press, Cambridge, Massachusetts.

Figure 1-5. Physical and Information Flows in a Production Organization

actual conditions is compared with the desired conditions and appropriate
corrective action initiated. The *apparent* state of actual conditions is considered because the information available at the decision point is an incomplete and only partly accurate reflection of the physical facts which it
represents. Thus an important aspect of any information system is how accurate and up-to-date are its descriptions of the physical world it represents.

Forrester's model illuminates two important aspects of information
systems: (1) information is an explicit and integral part of organizational
decision making (we have already pointed out that information derives its
value from its utilization in the decision process); and (2) information's
function is to represent the physical values of which the organization is
composed.

Synthesis—Dynamics and Hierarchy

In the models developed by Anthony, Simon, and Forrester, the decision process is central to their concepts of the organization. But each model emphasizes a different aspect of the roles of decisions and information. A synthesis of these views provides a more complete picture than any of them separately.

Forrester's description is unidimensional in the sense that no distinction is made between decision points except in terms of the functional areas to which their decisions relate. The result is a "flat" model with only one level. However, we can differentiate the decision points by their position in the organizational hierarchy as shown in figure 1-6. This figure emphasizes the fact that higher level decision points relay information to lower level points in the form of decisions and plans and allocate the resources for their realization. The recipients of resources then report back on their utilization.

Assume that the second level in figure 1-6 represents production management to which top management has given the task of producing 2,000 widgets and 1,000 gidgets with a budget of $50,000. This would be translated, say, into a plan for Shop 1 to produce 1,200 widgets with three widget machines and five men and for Shop 2 to produce 800 widgets and 1,000 gidgets with six men, two widget machines, and one gidget machine. The decision process in Shop 1 would then consist of allocating the men to machines and shifts and setting production targets for each machine/shift. The shop supervisor would report regularly on production to date and on any problems that might arise. Production management would in turn report on total production in both shops and on the relationship between planned and actual outlays.

In general, the higher in the organizational hierarchy the decision point, the less detailed will be the plans handed down, the more global the resource allocation, the less detailed the reports received, and the less programmed the decisions to be made. Thus a synthesis of the concept of the organization as a network of decision points together with the hierarchical concept provides a framework within which the types of decisions, the information entering into them, and the transformations undergone by the information all become explicit, as do the relationships between them.

Information Systems and Functional Organization

At the business (organic unit) level, organizations are usually divided into units specialized in terms of the functions they are to perform. Industrial firms, for example, have production, sales, finance, and personnel departments; the military has logistics, signals, combat, and medical units. It is

13

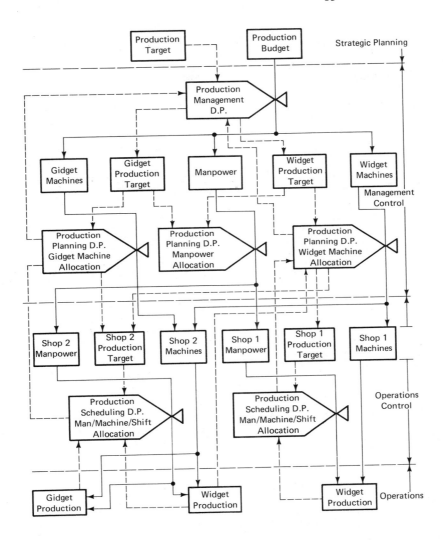

Figure 1-6. Hierarchical View of Industrial Dynamics

convenient to think of this as a vertical organization, because each function is represented at most levels of the organizational hierarchy. A partial example of the vertical organization is represented in figure 1-7.

A major problem in devising information systems is the fact that infor-- mation tends to ignore the vertical structure and flows back and forth across the boundaries of functional units. For example, production reports

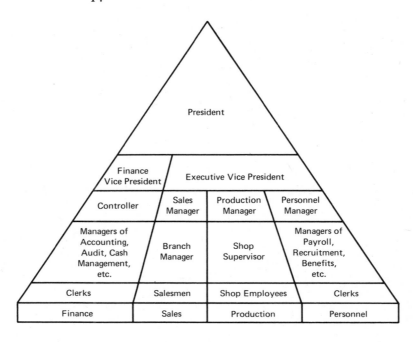

Figure 1-7. Schematic Example of Vertical Organization

to personnel on hours worked and on its manpower requirements; sales inquires from production on order status; finance informs other functions of the ratio of their actual to budgeted outlays. Because these interactions can take place at any level of the pyramid; a datum moving through the organization is quite likely to follow a horizontal course across several functional areas.

Designing an information system, then, requires the coordination of all the functional areas that provide and use the information in question. The system designer not only must be an expert on information systems, but also must understand the needs and problems of the various functions with which he comes into contact. Because no one person can know an entire organization in all its myriad detail, the information expert must know when to incorporate people from the functional areas into his design efforts.

Definition of a Management Information System

Until now we have dealt with information systems in general without trying to determine what makes such a system a *management* information system in particular. Unfortunately there are almost as many definitions of management information systems as there are people writing on the subject.

A representative sample of such definitions seems to cover two broad categories. Definitions in the first category place considerable emphasis on the physical realization of the system as one of the distinguishing features of an MIS. For example:

An information system may be defined as the procedures, methodologies, organization, software and hardware elements needed to insert and retrieve selected data as required for operating and managing a company.[5]

a management information system . . . is an integrated man-machine system for providing information to support operations, management, and decision making functions in the organization. The system utilizes computer hardware and software, manual procedures, management decision models, and a data base.[6]

an MIS is a system of people, equipment, procedures, documents, and communications that collects, validates, operates on, transforms, stores, retrieves and presents data for use in planning, budgeting, accounting, controlling and other management processes for various management purposes. . . . Information processing systems become management information systems as their purpose transcends a transaction processing orientation in favor of a management decision-making orientation.[7]

Definitions in the second category distinguish MIS entirely in terms of their functions in the organization, as the following four definitions show:

A management information system is designed to provide information needed to manage an organization.[8]

A management information system is an organized method of providing past, present and projection information relating to internal operations and external intelligence. It supports the planning, control and operational functions of an organization by furnishing information in the proper time frame to assist the decision maker.[9]

an information system consists of at least one PERSON of a certain PSYCHOLOGICAL TYPE who faces a PROBLEM within some ORGANIZATIONAL CONTEXT for which he needs EVIDENCE to arrive at a solution (i.e. to select some course of action) and that the evidence is made available to him through some MODE OF PRESENTATION.[10]

"management information systems" . . . a description for information processing activities in support of management.[11]

The word *computer* does not appear in any of this last group of definitions; in fact, there is no allusion whatsoever to the physical forms that management information systems may take. This is the principal feature separating this group of definitions from the previous group.

The first category of definitions is design-oriented because it defines an MIS in terms of its structure or design attributes. This approach is somewhat limiting, however. It is analogous to defining an airplane as a vehicle with wings and an engine that flies. Vehicles without these features are, therefore, not airplanes, regardless of whether they fly or not.

The second set of definitions defines an MIS as an information system that serves management rather than operations. This approach is use-oriented and states that a system is an MIS when it is used by a manager who finds it useful in the performance of his duties. This definition is analogous to the Turing test (named after the English mathematician and computer scientist who first suggested it) for artificial intelligence, which states that an artifact is intelligent when an intelligent human cannot distinguish its behavior from that of other intelligent humans. The analogy: managers are the touchstone for management information systems just as intelligent beings are the touchstone for intelligence.

Therefore, the definition of an MIS is an empirical issue that can be solved by observing the interactions of managers with information systems. Systems used by managers are management information systems; those which are not used by managers are not, no matter how sophisticated their design.

Many managers claim that they have management information systems. To their users, they are often of considerable practical value and certainly not mirages as claimed by Dearden. (Although Dearden denied the possibility of constructing an MIS because it required building an integrated model of the organization, none of the previous definitions in either group mention integration.[12]) Our definition of an MIS then:

 A management information system is a system for collecting, storing, retrieving, and processing information that is used, or desired, by one or more managers in the performance of their duties.

This criterion is somewhat ephemeral because what is an MIS for one manager may not be for another. Information systems do fall into disuse when managers change, indicating that our definition is valid. Thus an MIS is an MIS for a given manager with a given problem at a given time. This ambiguity causes some of the most serious problems in managing MIS and considerable attention is paid to it in this book.

Although our definition is not absolute, it does have the advantage of releasing the concept from technical considerations while founding it on functional criteria. Because the objective of an MIS is to perform certain functions rather than to fill given forms, this makes considerable sense.

Our definition also grants any information system the potential of becoming a management information system *should a manager find it useful and use it*. Thus, in one sense, there is very little to distinguish between MIS and information systems generally. In practice, however, the problem turns out to be precisely that of making systems attractive to potential users and eliciting a use response. The fact that this is so difficult to achieve is the reason that so many MIS fail. We must conclude, therefore, that there is some intrinsic difference between information systems generally and management information systems in particular. One of the aims of this book is to pin down this elusive essence of MIS.

An additional conclusion to be drawn from the definition is that an organization may have many MIS. Because many large organizations list scores and even hundreds of management information systems in their employ, it is limiting and misleading to speak of *the MIS* as if a firm can and should have only one such system. Much of the confusion in the debate over the feasibility of MIS stems from this misunderstanding.

Though we do not consider the technical characteristics of an information system useful in determining its managerial content, such characteristics do indicate the degree of sophistication and, to some extent, the potential value of an MIS. Furthermore, certain technical features seem to be common to most MIS.

Characteristics of Management Information Systems

The first characteristic of management information systems is that, like information systems in general, they collect, store, process, and output information. So do operational information systems or data-processing systems that perform routine clerical operations—the programmed activities described by Simon. Many MIS are in fact based on operational systems and evolve from them. As it becomes clear that the data stored in the operational system can be processed further to provide useful inputs for management decision making, additional capabilities are added. At some point the information system becomes sufficiently involved in managerial processes to justify the name MIS.

An MIS can be thought of as an interface between the data-processing and management-decision functions in the organization. The processed and stored data of the programmed clerical systems are one of the raw materials from which an MIS produces information appropriate for unprogrammed use at the managerial level. In terms of figure 1-6, MIS are responsible for collecting internal information from the lowest level decision points and pushing it up through the hierarchy.

To this point, the word *computer* has not yet appeared in our discussion of information systems. Management information systems existed before the invention of the digital computer, and there are manual systems that provide the necessary interface between operational and managerial processes.

Consider the following description of an eleventh-century manual information system:

Domesday is primarily a "geld book," that is a collection of facts made for a fiscal purpose, the proper collection of Danegeld. But although the questions asked and answered may have helped the collection of the geld, it is going too far to say that William the Conqueror could have had no further end in view. The final form in which the Domesday Book itself was laboriously recast out of the original returns, points to the other objects and ideas besides the Danegeld. The Book presents the King . . . an exact account of the power and resources of his feudatories and of their vassals in every shire.[13]

But given the quantity and complexity of data generated by modern enterprises, it is inconceivable that any but the smallest organizations could be capable of processing the data into decision inputs within a reasonable time. Thus the extensive use of electronic computers is one of the characteristics of modern management information systems. But the presence of an electronic data-processing system is by no means conclusive evidence that MIS are in operation.

Two major, and largely complementary, developments in the operations information system make possible its transformation into an MIS. The first is the concept of a data base, which is said to exist when the computerized files of an organization are integrated in such a way that any chain of logically related data items can be accessed as desired, regardless of physical residence and functional origin of the data. For example, consider a firm producing many products; associated with each product are production, inventory, and sales data. In the classic data-processing system, each type of information would be kept in a separate file and updated by inputs from the appropriate departments. Incorporating these files in a data base provides the ability to obtain all information relevant to the *product* from each of the files in which it is mentioned.

The second major development that transforms an operations system into an MIS is the use of the data in the system in models of the organization. The models in question may be either analytic optimization models, such as the linear programming models used extensively in the oil refining industry, or heuristic, such as the simulation models used for projecting the traffic handling capabilities of transportation facilities.

In theory, and often in practice, the data base and models may be developed independently. But the two are highly complementary in the sense that the existence of a data base makes it easier for the model builder to learn the parameters and obtain the inputs he needs for his models. On the other hand, because the regular use of sophisticated models is one of the ultimate goals of the MIS, the development of models indicates the kinds of data that should be incorporated in the data base and the relationships between them.

A final element common to many management information systems is the use of time sharing to permit interaction between the decision maker and the information system. Time sharing allows the decision maker to continue retrieving information until he finds exactly what he wants or to run a model many times with different inputs to compare the effect of changing assumptions on the result. In this manner the manager can run a series of experiments dictated by a chain of thought without losing time between one experiment and the next.

In conclusion, the physical MIS is usually composed of a computerized data processing system in which the data files have been integrated into a data base to produce answers to complex queries. An advanced MIS will usually include a number of models of organizational activities to facilitate decision making and will probably allow direct interaction between the manager and the system.

Successful Management Information Systems

Surveys of companies using computer systems show that they can be divided readily into two groups—successful and unsuccessful. Surprisingly, the distinction is quite clear. Partial success does not often occur.

To prepare the reader to play a part in bringing about successful MIS, we must define success. Among the criteria for a successful MIS are profitability, performance, application areas, user satisfaction, and degree of use.

Profitability

The evaluation and achievement of profitability is a major problem in MIS. Achieving profitability is also a serious problem with operations systems in which costs tend to outrun projections and benefits tend to fall short. But at least the evaluation of effectiveness is relatively simple because costs are known and benefits take the form of savings of clerical personnel and are also readily measurable.

With management systems, cost evaluation is still reasonably simple, but evaluating effectiveness becomes virtually impossible because benefits take the form of improved performance of the organization rather than concrete savings. It thus becomes very difficult to determine whether benefits outweigh costs and considerable experience or intuition may be necessary.

Performance

The justification for MIS is that they improve the performance of managers—that is, they improve the quality of managers' decisions. Like profitability, it is difficult to measure to what extent performance has indeed improved; the higher the level of the decision and the longer the time over which it takes effect, the more difficult this becomes. Evidence may be provided, however, by managers' subjective feelings about the effects of the systems on their performance and from the observations of their superiors.

Areas of Application

One condition for a successful MIS is that it be applied to major problems of the organization. A system, no matter how sophisticated, can hardly have an impact sufficient to justify its cost if it is applied to areas of marginal concern to the organization. Surveys show that attacking major issues is an important characteristic of successful systems.

✓ User Satisfaction

User satisfaction is a frankly subjective evaluation of the system by those it is designed to assist. Managers who use a system may be dissatisfied either because the system fails to fulfill its functions or, at least, fails to fulfill the users' expectations of it. User satisfaction, however, is prima facie evidence that the system is successful.

Widespread Use

This indicator also depends on the feelings of users toward the system. In fact, we consider it the most significant criterion because a manager will use a system intensively only if it meets at least some of the previous criteria. Furthermore, it fits our own definition, which states that it is use by a manager that makes an information system an MIS.

Using these criteria, we can define a successful MIS as one that is profitably applied to an area of major concern to the organization, is widely used by one or more satisfied managers, and improves the quality of their performance. Although most of our criteria are subjective, managerial use is the acid test for MIS. The decision to use an MIS is based on the manager's subjective evaluation of its effectiveness.

Summary

Information has two roles in organizations. As raw data, it is generated by and participates in the operations of the organization. After processing, it may participate in management decision making. In this role, information serves as a surrogate for the reality of the organization, which is too complex to be encompassed by any single person. In parallel with the hierarchy of control processes in organizations there is a hierarchy of decision processes—from completely programmed to completely nonprogrammed—and a hierarchy of the degree of processing required of information—from raw unprocessed data to the highly aggregated and processed information input to analytical models and high level decisions.

Management information systems collect, store, process, and output information that is used by management. Often they accept operational data as inputs and, by processing, transform it into managerial information. In the modern environment, such systems are almost invariably computer-based and include the use of analytic decision models, large-scale data bases, and time-sharing technologies.

We define a management information system as an information system used by one or more managers who consider it useful in the performance of their duties. A successful MIS is profitably applied to an area of major concern to the organization, is widely used by one or more satisfied managers, and improves the quality of their performance. Widespread use is the most significant indicator of success.

Notes

1. Robert N. Anthony, *Planning and Control Systems: A Framework for Analysis* (Boston: Division of Research, Graduate School of Business Administration, Harvard University, 1965). (Italics in the original.)

2. Herbert A. Simon, *The New Science of Management Decision*, rev. ed. (Englewood Cliffs, N.J.: Prentice-Hall, 1977).

3. Jay W. Forrester, *Industrial Dynamics* (Cambridge, Mass.: M.I.T. Press, 1961).

4. Jay W. Forrester, "Managerial Decision Making," in *Computers and the World of the Future* ed. Martin Greenberger. (Cambridge, Mass.: M.I.T. Press, 1962), pp. 36-99.

5. A. F. Moravec, "Basic Concepts For Designing A Fundamental Information System," *Management Services*, vol. II, no. 4 (July-August 1965), pp. 37-45.

6. Gordon B. Davis, *Management Information Systems: Conceptual Foundations, Structure and Development* (New York: McGraw-Hill, 1974).

7. M. K. Schwartz, "MIS Planning," *Datamation*, vol. 16, no. 10 (September 1970), pp. 28-31.

8. J. C. Emery, "Management Information Systems" in *Progress in Operations Research*, vol. 3, ed. Julius Aronofsky. (New York: Wiley, 1969).

9. Walter Kenneron, "MIS Universe," *Data Management* (September 1970).

10. R. O. Mason, and I. I. Mitroff, "A Program for Research on Management Information Systems." *Management Science*, vol. 19, no. 5 (January 1973), pp. 475-487.

11. Charles H. Kriebel, "MIS Technology—A View of the Future," *Proceedings of the Spring Joint Computer Conference* (1972), pp. 1173-80.

12. John Dearden, "MIS is a Mirage." *Harvard Business Review*, vol. 50, no. 1 (January-February 1972), pp. 90-99.

13. G. M. Trevelyan, *History of England*, vol. 1 (New York: Doubleday, 1952).

Suggested Readings

Anthony, Robert N. *Planning and Control Systems: A Framework for Analysis.* Boston: Division of Research, Graduate School of Business Administration, Harvard University, 1965.

Dearden, John. "MIS Is a Mirage." *Harvard Business Review,* vol. 50, no. 1 (January-February 1972), pp. 90-99.

Forrester, Jay W. *Industrial Dynamics.* Cambridge, Mass.: M.I.T. Press, 1961.

Hanold, Terrance. "An Executive View of MIS." *Datamation*, vol. 18, no. 11 (November 1972), pp. 65-71.

Mason, R. O., and Mitroff, I. I. "A Program for Research on Management Information Systems." *Management Science*, vol. 19, no. 5 (January 1973), pp. 475-487.

Simon, Herbert A. *The New Science of Management Decision*, rev. ed. Englewood Cliffs, N.J.: Prentice-Hall, 1977.

2 The MIS Environment

Before beginning work on an MIS project, it is extremely important to evaluate the environment in which it will be implemented. This environment is a combination of factors both inside and outside the organization that determine the state of the world in which the MIS operates or will operate and with which it interacts.

The environment will be conducive to success if it provides a suitable climate and necessary resources. Some organizations or extraorganizational situations, however, produce hostile climates or circumscribe resource availability in ways that retard or depress the MIS effort.

The situational variables must be evaluated before undertaking a project. If the evaluation shows the environment to be favorable, further steps can be taken with little fear. On the other hand, it may be very risky to initiate an MIS in an unfavorable environment that cannot be changed or neutralized. Unsuccessful cases of information system development often show that the effort was doomed to failure before it even began because the environment was completely unsupportive. This situation may be obvious in advance, if one makes the necessary inquiries.

Some environmental factors that a priori might appear to be very important turn out in practice to be of little import. Some important factors are not at all obvious and come to light only after analyzing a number of cases.

Size of the Organization

No evidence indicates that small companies have more difficulty with information systems than do large organizations; in fact, there are some indications that the opposite may be true. But small organizations certainly face different types of problems than large companies.

The first problem imposed on smaller organizations by information systems is the amount of resources required. Although the considerable economies of scale inherent in computer operations have become less pronounced since the advent of minicomputers many times more powerful than the medium-size computer of ten years ago and at a fraction of the cost, significant indivisibilities in programming and operations still make systems relatively greater burdens on smaller companies than on larger organizations.

The resource drain caused by information systems can seriously affect the financial situation of a small company, whereas this is unlikely to be the case in larger organizations. As a result, small organizations may attempt to trim costs by acquiring underpowered hardware or by understaffing. The financial burden may also lead to pressures for quick results, which, combined with understaffing and insufficient hardware, can quickly lead to failure.

In smaller organizations especially, the effects on cash flow and overall financial situation must be carefully considered in addition to the profitability of a system. Projects should be undertaken only if they are economically sound and feasible. The risks are clearly greater in smaller organizations.

The second problem is that smaller organizations tend to have less formal structures and procedures, as a number of phenomena signify a tendency to bypass middle management, because the president may be able, or thinks he is able, to control everything—especially in the entrepreneurial or family firm; consequent lack of control and coordination between units and a tendency for each department to do things its own way; and a tendency to make decisions intuitively rather than analytically.

Because effective MIS entail systematizing the relevant decision process, considerable effort may need to be expended in formalizing and rationalizing the organization. Size alone usually forces a large organization to formalize its procedures. All firms, especially smaller companies, should beware of the tendency to solve organizational problems by installing information systems. This is putting the cart before the horse; the organization must put its house in order if MIS are to have a chance to succeed.

The need to systematize before developing systems and the relative scarcity of resources will generally result in a longer lead time for MIS in small organizations than in large. Size, however, also has its disadvantages—particularly its association with complexity and diversity. Clearly, the more complex and diverse the systems to be developed, the greater the difficulty involved. The solution seems to be careful definition of the system before beginning implementation. Many systems have failed under the weight of complications not seen in advance, unplanned for, and therefore detrimental.

Structure of the Organization

The one aspect of organizational structure whose impact on the MIS has been documented is the degree of centralization of the organization. Centralization, or decentralization, of the organization and its effects on the implementation and functioning of the information system is a variable referred to quite frequently in the MIS literature.

A word of caution, however, may be useful. Centralization with respect to an MIS may imply the centralization of one, some, or all of five different elements:

1. The degree of centralization of the organization in which the MIS is implemented
2. The degree of centralization of the MIS development and implementation efforts
3. The degree of centralization of the MIS unit
4. The degree of centralization of the computer resource
5. The degree of centralization of the system's data base

Because few concepts are used, misused, and confused in the context of management information systems as much as "centralization," it is of great importance to identify clearly which aspect is meant at any given time. In this chapter we will discuss the first aspect—the degree of centralization of the organization in which the MIS is implemented.

Decentralized companies are constantly changing. They grow, become more complex and more widely dispersed geographically. This evolution has accelerated in the seventies and is expected to increase even more in the next decade. Such changes have magnified the problems of control in decentralized corporations. Management of decentralized divisions is, by definition, top management. Thus the management problems encountered are strategic (rather than operational), usually unstructured, and nonrecurrent. Problems of this type do not lend themselves easily to computerized or mathematical solutions. Some authorities believe, therefore, that because of the nature of control in decentralized companies and its increased complexity, the development of the new information technology has been of little help in managing them.

Although this pessimism seems somewhat extreme to us, developing MIS for decentralized companies poses very definite difficulties. The major problem is to ensure that the systems built by different divisions can communicate with one another; otherwise the firm may find itself with a number of independent systems that cannot be aggregated or compared. The organization can then no longer produce a consolidated picture of itself as a whole, with consequent danger of loss of control. A good example of the issues involved is provided by a case report on the Weyerhaeuser Company, in which parallel systems were developed in three groups of the company.[1] Maximum use of common data files for all systems and compatibility of the different systems were emphasized so that they would form a corporate management information system.

Organizational Time Frame

Time is a critical element in the decision-making process, especially in managerial decision making. Among the factors that may affect the time frame in different organizations are (1) the culture in which the organization is embedded, (2) the industry, and (3) the size of the organization.

In some countries, time is not money to the same extent that it is in the United States, partly because rates of change and development are slower. Because the environment changes only slowly, firms in such countries do not need to react as quickly as do those in more dynamic environments. But even where the environment is dynamic, cultural factors may dictate different styles of decision making with slower time frames. Japan is a classic example of the second case; an article on business customs in Japan indicates that decision making there is much more drawn out because of a culturally determined preference for consensus decisions.[2] Once decisions are taken, however, execution tends to be rapid and trouble-free because of the prior consensus. Decision making in the United States by comparison tends to be fast and authoritarian; this difference leads to problems and delays in execution, which in turn require rapid decisions.

The technical characteristics of an industry and the nature of competition in it also have considerable influence on the company's time frame. Rapidly changing technologies can dictate a need for fast decisions; for example, compare the rates of change in the electronics industry to those in the commercial aircraft industry and the resulting effects on decision time frames. Similarly, if a company faces little or no competition it may allow itself a more leisurely pace of decision making than if the situation is highly competitive; for example, supermarkets have to make faster decisions than such public utilities as electric or telephone companies.

Finally, smaller companies are more likely to be pressed into short decision cycles than larger ones. The growth rate in small companies is likely to be much higher than in more mature firms, so that the changes required will tend to be more frequent and more urgent. Furthermore, when faced by competition or technological change, small firms cannot afford to let themselves get behind because they lack the resources to ride out periods of declining demand; large corporations, however, often absorb the effects of complacency with little harm.

The significance of the organizational time frame for MIS is that it is much more difficult to mount a successful information systems effort when the time frame is highly constrained than when it is more relaxed. Two factors cause this state of affairs. The first is the subjective attitudes of system implementors towards the problem of organizational time frame. The second is the length of time objectively required to implement information system projects.

Writing on the problems of applying management science techniques, Grayson succinctly presents the attitudinal problem in terms that apply equally to the application of management information systems.[3] He argues that management scientists are not aware of the time constraints on managerial decision making. They operate in a time frame that is slower than that of the executives and apply the same painstaking methods, no matter what the exigencies of the situation. Thus, managers simply tend to pass them by when pressing problems require rapid solutions.

Even when the implementors are attuned to the time pressures under which management operates, the length of time objectively required to construct the system may render it obsolete before it is completed. For example, in a large petroleum company, all the details on the construction of the model were agreed on, but the project was discontinued after four years, still incomplete. A large aerospace corporation succeeded in building a corporate planning model, but then found that its staff were unable to keep the data up to date, nor were they able to utilize it effectively because of its size and inflexibility. These problems are typically encountered in attempting to use comprehensive management information systems. First, the data take so long to collect that often they have outlived their usefulness before all are in hand. Second, the models often take so long to produce results that they are of little interest by the time they are made available.

The time-frame problem is further complicated by the rapid change that often characterizes modern organizations. The fact that companies and their information needs are changing very rapidly would make it difficult for information systems to keep up in the best of circumstances. But the problems associated with incongruence of time frames between implementors and users lead to many cases in which information systems simply do not keep pace with management needs. MIS executives have to run very hard indeed if they want to provide information that is timely enough to be useful.

Organizational Maturity

The next factor in the organizational environment is the maturity of the organization. Like its size, structure, and time factors, the maturity of the organization helps to shape the environment in which the MIS will operate and so also has a share in determining success and failure. The more mature an organization, the greater the likelihood that management information systems will succeed.

In discussing organizational maturity, it is useful to think of organizations as complex, man-made systems. Unlike most man-made systems, few organizations are the product of detailed advance planning; instead, they evolve over time with no clearly defined blueprint to guide them. Processes, products, departments, functions, and positions are added and deleted; interrelationships are created and eliminated; structures are developed and changed. Like any living organism, organizations are in a constant state of flux.

As a result of this process, or simply as a result of the complexity of operations, many organizational systems are "black boxes," whose inputs and outputs are observable, but whose internal workings are obscured, even to their managers. Technologies are applied because they work, without being really understood. Routine and inertia create patterns of action that are not always clear or obvious. Thus many organization systems are poorly defined and not well understood, do not lend themselves to quantitative analysis, and do not process or produce data that are relevant to decision making in the organization. These organizations are immature, often defending their systems with "That's the way we've always done it!"

Mature organizations, on the other hand, are those in which systems are well understood, well defined, and quantified and which produce data appropriate to their decision and control processes.

Organizational maturity is not necessarily associated with the age of the organization. An old established organization, whose systems have been complicated by generations of ad hoc changes, may be, according to our definition, quite immature. A new, well-designed organization may, on the other hand, commence activity with a high level of maturity. However, old firms in stable industries usually tend to be more mature than young firms in growth industries.

Understanding

To construct a useful description of an organization, it must be sufficiently well understood so that the relevant variables can be identified. If a model is under consideration, relationships between the variables must be clearly understood.

The level of understanding often depends on the industry to which a firm belongs. In old, technologically stable industries such as basic chemicals, oil refining, or steel, the production processes have been thoroughly studied and are well understood. The same is true, to some extent, of marketing processes in industries that have been widely researched—supermarkets, for example.

Age of an industry is no guarantee of understanding, however. An interesting example is the automation of process control in the paper manufacturing industry in the 1960s. Before automation could be undertaken, several years were devoted to studying the processes that had previously not been sufficiently understood and whose parameters had not been defined. If this is the case with many ancient industries, it is natural that in new, technologically dynamic, or unresearched industries, processes may be less well understood.

If the technological aspects of organizations present such problems, it is no wonder that administrative and management processes with their behavioral elements and dependence on human factors such as personality and intuition are often little understood even by those participating in them. Only if such understanding is achieved, however, can we consider the organization to be mature.

Quantification

The construction of formal information systems requires not only that processes be well understood, but that they also be presented in a form suitable for processing and analysis, which usually implies quantitative rather than qualitative description. In many cases, such descriptions originate in accounting systems and develop through budgeting and financial planning systems. Other quantitative descriptions originate from the collection and storage of data in the production and marketing functions. Considerable effort may be required to transform an organization from ill-defined, qualitative approaches to well-defined, quantitative thinking. Such a transition is essential if an organization is to be considered mature.

Data Availability

Systems can be quantified only if data are both available and accessible. Both aspects are important. First, some of the data required for decision analysis simply may not have been collected in the past or may be available only in a form unsuitable for use without considerable revision. Second, the desired data often exist somewhere in the organization, but they are of little use because of the difficulty entailed in actually putting them together.

It has been found that if data needed for an analysis require extensive compilation or are buried in some other part of the organization, managers are most likely to forego the analysis rather than retrieve the data for two reasons: (1) data collection and massage can consume lengthy periods of time and decisions often cannot be delayed for that long (remember the organizational time frame!) and (2) when data are under someone else's jurisdiction, the negotiations required to obtain them may make the whole exercise seem not worth the effort.

In conclusion, organizational maturity depends on the existence and accessibility of data as well as on understanding and quantification. In organizations lacking these indications of maturity, it is much more difficult to construct successful MIS.

Resource Availability

Resource availability problems frequently contribute to the failure of management information systems for two major reasons. First, the MIS function must compete with other functions in the organization for whatever resources are available. The competition at this level is for slices of the organizational pie, expressed primarily as budgetary allocations. Usually, requests for budget appropriations are justified by showing that expected incomes, or savings, exceed the cost of the program for which the budget is requested. This process can be a major difficulty for MIS projects because the benefits tend to be very difficult to estimate in monetary terms. The principal purpose of MIS is to improve managerial decision making; how does one measure an improvement in managerial performance and how much is it worth? The inability to answer this question at any but the lowest levels of management is one of the most significant problems of the practice and theory of MIS. It has generated much research, little of it yet with direct practical applicability in the fields of information theory, statistical decision theory, and team theory. We hope that research in these areas will eventually provide tools for evaluating the contribution of MIS to the profitability of businesses and the efficiency of nonbusiness organizations. (This discussion of the evaluation problem is expanded in chapter 3.)

Obtaining budgetary allocations for the MIS is further complicated by the fact that the information function is not generally perceived to be in the forefront of the organizations' activities in the same way as production, marketing, and finance. The MIS is often regarded as a support function that is often cut back first during a profit squeeze or tight money period. Only after information systems have become well established and the organization depends on them do they achieve a significant position in organizational priorities.

The second resource problem of the MIS is the translation of the budget into such physical resources as equipment, managers, and technicians. Equipment usually presents no great difficulty; many manufacturers offer a vast variety of data processing systems.

However, obtaining the right people is the major problem. Good programmers and analysts are often hard to find and even harder to keep. According to McFarlan, one company's MIS took four and a half years to become operational because of a shortage of analyst-programmers.[4] In many cases, project leaders and other information system managers are the constraining resource, particularly in companies planning a rapid expansion in information systems; project leaders are often spread too thin to permit work to proceed on a broad front. The result is inevitably a slowdown in progress because technical personnel do not get the leadership they require. In another case cited by McFarlan, planning horizons were stretched from three to five years because of a shortage of managerial personnel.[5] Unutilized budgets for key MIS personnel are common.

For the organization planning an MIS effort and for the MIS leaders particularly, it is vital to tailor projects to the available financial and human resources. Unless such planning occurs, the MIS unit can have many projects in process stretched over a long period of time, but with very little progress visible to the rest of the organization. This common situation quickly leads to talk of MIS failure and possible budgetary cutbacks, which slow things down even further (the organizational time frame raises its head again!). MIS commitments should not be made without ensuring that the required resources are available immediately and for the planned duration of the project.

Psychological Climate

Each organization develops a unique psychological climate, which is set by the dominant view of management information systems held by its members. Such expectations, preconceptions, and attitudes are affected by experience with and information about MIS, including rumors or reports on experience with MIS in other organizations, past personal experience of members of the organization, sales pitches of computer salesmen and consultants, and even college courses on information systems. In organizations that have already implemented information systems, the manner in which the implementation was executed also strongly affects the psychological climate.

Organizational expectations have to tread a straight and narrow path. On one hand, high expectations have been identified as an essential precondition for outstanding MIS performance; on the other, excessive expectations contribute to MIS failure.

High expectations can be both self-induced or fostered by computer, operations research, and MIS experts, leading management to expect much more of information systems than can be produced. Managers can mislead themselves into expecting too much of information systems when, overburdened by the influx of problems requiring solutions, they attempt to turn over some of their functions to the MIS. (This expedient seems to be reasonable because many other managerial responsibilities are successfully delegated to lower ranks or to specialists.) Thus managers sometimes think that after a short briefing in which the needs and goals of the MIS are stated, the MIS experts will withdraw and in due time will present management with a solution. In the extreme version of this approach, management feels that most complicated business problems can be stated mathematically, the specialists develop a computerized version of the mathematical model, and the manager, seated at a terminal keyboard, makes decisions based on the outputs of the model.

According to these expectations, the manager states problems and the specialist provides solutions; the choice of solution and final decision is the prerogative of the manager. The fallacy in this approach—that managers need not be closely involved in all phases of information system development—has been demonstrated countless times in practice (it is also the main theme of chapter 5, which deals with the responsibilities of executives in the MIS context). As a result, most surveys of executives, even in the most advanced companies, convey a feeling that computers have been oversold or at least overbought. This feeling is only a short step away from the conclusion that management information systems are a failure.

Managers' high expectations of information systems, however, are not created spontaneously. They are often fostered by computer, operations research, and MIS specialists. As professionals, these specialists do not view themselves as substitutes for managers or even as partners in management. They desire well-defined, unchanging decision problems to which they may apply their expertise and produce solutions. Managers are led to expect that redefinition and clarification are part of the specialists' work that will lead to better solutions than those developed in the past by experience and intuition. In fact, formalizing a problem frequently requires simplification to the point where many elements are ignored and there is little resemblance between the problem solved by the information system and that presented by the real world—clearly circumstances in which a manager's expectations may be disappointed.

Information system specialists further contribute to exaggerated expectations by underestimating the effort required for system development. Overoptimistic schedules, wishful thinking about the flexibility of systems, and overambitious plans for data-base development and integration of systems often result in the definition of infeasible programs. When progress lags far behind anticipations, frustration and feelings of failure are generated.

On the other hand, the obverse error sometimes occurs when the experts, fearful of creating exaggerated expectations, play down the possibilities of MIS. Their expectations may be so uninspiring that they dampen enthusiasm and deter managers from making demands; in fact, they may convince them that it is not worth their while to become involved. Horror stories about MIS use in other organizations may also contribute to this lowered set of expectations. People with bad experiences with MIS, especially those who do not understand what really happened but who merely witness the end result, can effectively depress others' expectations.

An important function of MIS management is the creation of a realistic level of expectations in the organization that is neither too high nor too low. A realistic picture can be drawn by avoiding overblown forecasts for savings in clerical and management personnel, by carefully reassessing sky-high rate-of-return projections, and by abstaining from promising up-to-the-minute data and totally integrated systems. On the positive side, the capabilities and limitations of systems should be clearly stated; tangible and intangible benefits should be carefully discussed and understood; and schedules and investments should be conservatively but realistically estimated.

The MIS manager's task of creating realistic expectations regarding information systems can be affected by preconceptions in the organization. In some cases, executives develop strong preconceptions about what the MIS should be like—its structure, modes of operation, use, goals, or even output formats. Managers may even identify these preconceptions with their own style of management. In such circumstances, alternatives proposed by the experts may be rejected simply because they do not conform to managers' preconceptions.

Such preconceptions are also closely associated with such common expectations about MIS as "The computer can't give you any more than you put into it" or, at the other extreme, that if the system cannot provide the manager with every bit of information he wants at precisely the moment he wants it, then he doesn't really need it. Such preconceptions clearly can distort the expectations held by the organization about information systems. The weaker the preconceptions, the better the chances of creating realistic expectations.

Once an MIS has been installed, the psychological climate is also affected by perceptions, attitudes, and experience with the system. Lucas, who examined these variables in several studies found that attitudes and perceptions of MIS are determined by the quality of the system. Good experience generates favorable attitudes and encourages widespread use.[6] Bad experience has the opposite effect. Because widespread use is one of our criteria for the success of an MIS (chapter 1), attitudes clearly play an important role in determining success.

Both the quality of an MIS and attitudes toward it are affected by prior expectations. High but reasonable expectations motivate the construction of high-quality systems. Low expectations permit the approval of unambitious projects. On the other hand, expectations modulate the effect of system quality on attitudes; where expectations are high, only high-quality systems will be satisfying, and low-quality systems will engender unfavorable attitudes. Where expectations are low, even a mediocre system may be a pleasant surprise and lead to favorable attitudes. This network of interrelationships may be summarized as in figure 2-1.

The manager of information services thus can influence the success of his systems by his influence on the psychological climate in the organization. If he allows exaggerated expectations to develop, it will be difficult to build systems that meet them, and disappointment will follow. If he is satisfied with low expectations, he may be able to get away with poor systems for a time, but in the long run someone will probably take a hard look and ask embarassing questions. Only if realistically high expectations are developed will reasonably good systems be demanded and accepted.

Nature of the Problems

Managerial problems differ widely. Multinational corporations face different problems than provincial companies; government agencies encounter management and control problems unlike those in the private economy; airlines attain effectivity through processes that do not apply to universities or the electronics industry; production management differs from marketing or personnel management.

These differences spill over into management information systems. Some problems lend themselves more readily to the assistance of formal information systems than others. Obviously, the probability of successfully completing MIS projects is greater when the nature of the problem lends itself to solution by MIS.

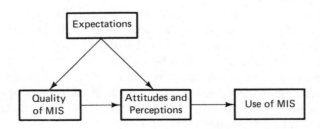

Figure 2-1. Role of Attitudes in MIS Success

The nature of the problem is a product of four factors:

1. the industry in which the problem arises
2. the level of management to which the problem refers
3. the functional area of the organization which is responsible for solving the problem
4. the time frame of the problem

Each factor can render a problem more, or less, amenable to formalization.

The Industry Factor

Industries that face structured problems or quantifiable problems with information-based solutions lend themselves more readily to computerized assistance in problem solving than do industries in which decision processes are more intuitive and judgmental. Railroads, airlines, utilities, oil-refining, steel, food, and timber-products companies tend to be of the first type. In some cases, such as oil refining and breweries, models have been built that encompass a large proportion of the activities of some companies; the ability to construct models is prima facie evidence of the tractability of such industries to problem solving by information systems. In other industries, such as investment banking, medicine, oil exploration, and book publishing, computerized systems can do little more than provide basic data that can be translated into viable decisions only by applying experience and intuition.

The Level of Management Factor

In the previous chapter we discussed the tendency for decision problems to become less structured, less routine, and less quantifiable the higher one goes in the managerial hierarchy. Harlan D. Mills has formulated this law as "The Bigger The Problem, The Fewer The Facts."[7]

As a result, many problems at lower management levels can be thoroughly studied and solved analytically. At the top executive level, on the other hand, so much uncertainty is involved and so much information lacking that it is difficult to make any decisions at all, let alone optimal ones. Some authorities believe that, no matter how much progress is made with MIS, some areas will always remain outside their domain. Certainly, the MIS approach has not been attempted or has not been successful in many decision areas. Thus the aspiring manager of MIS should be prepared to encounter and identify such problems and, above all, to admit frankly when he has no assistance to offer; it is preferable to bear the short-lived (and cheap) embarrassment of such an admission rather than the long-lasting (and expensive) embarrassment of an unsuccessful system.

The Functional Area Factor

Some functional areas encounter problems that are more favorable to the MIS approach than others. For example, many information systems have been successfully applied in production management, finance, and accounting functions. The marketing function is somewhat less amenable to computerization, but progress has been made in simulating advertising mix and scheduling and new product situations to suggest alternative outcomes as a basis for decisions. Virtually no progress has been made in decision systems for personnel, research, or investment management. Hospital management is an interesting example of problem differentiation, MIS assistance has been much more effective in outpatient than in inpatient applications where "both the organization and the medical vocabulary used are far more demanding than in the outpatient setting."[8]

To some extent, the functional area and industry factors interact. The same problem may be far more suitable for formalization in some industries than in others. As PoKempner points out, logistics and inventory control procedures have been thoroughly researched.[9] For the government, with its enormous procurement programs of standardized items, such procedures are clearly advantageous. For a small, dynamic, civilian program with frequently changing items, rigid standardized procedures may hinder more than they help.

The Time Frame Factor

We previously indicated that the organizational time frame differs among organizations and that it can have a considerable impact on the success of MIS. Here we deal with the variance in time frame between different problems within the same organization.

For example, a survey of hospital information systems found that much higher levels of system integration have been achieved in ambulatory medical facilities than in inpatient facilities.[10] The principal reason for this is that outpatient treatment poses simpler problems with more relaxed time frames.

Thus the problem time frame is also associated with the level of management to which it is delegated. The more important a decision, the more data are relevant to it, and the longer it takes to collect, process and evaluate the data: "a major decision, by the time it is supported by a sound factual basis, in all likelihood, should have been made several years ago."[11]

Thus, a difficult dilemma is created. On the one hand, it is easier to build systems when the problem cycle has a relaxed time frame. On the other hand, some of the most satisfactory and therefore successful applications are real-time systems that have been implemented to resolve needs for almost instantaneous reaction—for example, in military command and control systems, airport traffic control systems, and industrial process control. Such systems, however, are much more difficult to construct and therefore more likely to terminate as costly failures. A major problem facing MIS managers is to identify and undertake projects that promise assistance in areas with constrained time frames, where the contribution is consequently significant. On the other hand, they should be careful not to promise results when the time frame is so rigid as to impose unrealistic response times.

The Extraorganizational Situation

In addition to the organization's internal environment—its size, structure, time frame, maturity, resource availability, psychological climate, and problem types—the MIS also interacts directly with some features of the firm's external environment, especially resources that are not available within the firm itself. Specifically, such extraorganizational resources include decision techniques, software and hardware technology, and data-processing personnel.

Decision Techniques

As Ansoff points out, management technology, not data processing, is the limiting factor on the application of computers to management.[12] Operations research techniques are still limited to well-structured problems with analytical solutions. Most nontrivial real-world problems are not well structured; although they may sometimes be reduced to some canonical form, such simplification frequently means there is little resemblance between the model and the reality it is supposed to represent. Thus, although constant progress is being made in the development and application of mathematical models to decision problems, managers cannot simply assume that a solution exists. Before making a commitment to an MIS that is dependent on a scientific decision technique, they should determine whether an appropriate technique exists and whether it is feasible to apply it in the particular case being considered—especially managers in organizations that do not have their own management science department and so are completely dependent on solutions generally available in the environment.

Software Technology

One aspect of software technology is directly connected with the issue of management technology. It is not sufficient that a decision technique exist for it to be useful, but it must also be translated into an *algorithm* and programmed for a computer in such a way as to solve problems of a magnitude relevant to real situations. (An algorithm is an effective procedure for solving a problem or computing a quantity.) For example, linear programming was mastered as a mathematical technique quite some time before the computing and programming technologies were sufficient to solve realistically large problems. At present, considerable work is being done on devising reasonably efficient integer programming algorithms, an area in which the amount of computation required is still a real constraint. The absence of effective, off-the-shelf computer programs has been quoted as a brake on the adoption of advanced decision techniques by management.[13]

The second aspect of software technology is closely related to the first, but is somewhat wider in scope. It does not restrict itself to the question of whether a particular decision technique is programmable but rather asks whether *any* procedure is available for a given task that one wishes to implement in the MIS. Although software production is making great strides, and new programming packages are constantly being made available, our ability to envisage new systems tends to outrun our ability to program them.

A good current example relates to data base management and communications, two areas which have developed rapidly in recent years. After developing a data base it is quite natural for an organization to desire its interrogation from remote locations; many data-base management systems, however, do not include this option. Thus a firm may find itself with a data base and with a communications system, but then discover that the two are incompatible.

Software technologies have made such great advances in recent years that one begins to assume that anything can be done; perhaps this is true, but often a considerable amount of time and effort are required. Thus, it is essential to determine the availability of all the requisite programming packages, or the ability to produce them, before undertaking projects that require advanced software.

Hardware Technology

This issue is very similar to that of software technology. Software technology has been developing very rapidly and it is fairly safe to say that advances in hardware have been even more rapid. Nevertheless, some conceptual systems can be designed that are infeasible for existing hardware. Some areas that require careful evaluation are the amount of direct access storage required on-line, response times from direct access storage units, the load on communications networks, the availability of terminals human engineered for specific applications, and the sensitivity of the equipment to environmental conditions. Just as the availability of software should be carefully considered, the availability of necessary hardware should also be established before commitments are made to advanced projects.

Personnel

MIS authorities generally agree that one of the scarcest resources in the field is good personnel with adequate training in such MIS-related occupations as data processing, management science, and project management. It has been stated that "brainware" rather than hardware or software has been the effective constraint on the development of advanced management information systems.[14]

McFarlan cites a financial services company that was interested in the development of a new application with high profit potential.[15] It was estimated, however, that it would be impossible to develop the system with manpower then available and it would be necessary to recruit people from outside the organization. The company found that the complexity of the system was such that newly recruited people, even with appropriate backgrounds, would require two years of training before they became effective on the project. Thus total project development time was estimated as requiring four and a half years. Many MIS development projects find themselves dependent in this way on the external environment of the organization and on the manpower available in it.

The larger the project and the more people required, the more likely that insufficient manpower will be available within the organization and it will be necessary to recruit externally. Given the shortage of appropriately trained people and the long training periods required for externally recruited personnel, long-range recruitment plans are highly beneficial.

The main points made in this chapter and their implications for MIS management are summarized in table 2-1.

Table 2-1
Summary of MIS Environmental Variables

Variables	*Conclusions*
Organizational size	Small organizations are as likely to succeed with MIS as large organizations.
	In smaller organizations, MIS may impose a relatively heavier drain on resources. Therefore, cash flow and financial situation must be carefully considered.
	The lead time for MIS development will generally be longer in smaller organizations.
Organizational structure	Decentralized organizations should ensure that systems developed in the various divisions are compatible and can communicate with one another.
Organizational time frame	The organizational time frame is determined by culture, industry, and size.
	It is more difficult to construct successful MIS when the organizational time frame is short.
	MIS managers should be aware of the tendency for their time frames to exceed those of the organization; efforts should be made to synchronize the information system time frame with that of the organization.
Organizational maturity	Organizational maturity is determined by the understanding of organizational processes, the ability to quantify those processes, and the availability of relevant data.
	It is more difficult to construct successful MIS in immature organizations than in mature ones.
Resource availability	The development of MIS requires budgets sufficient for equipment, software, and technical personnel.
	Projects should be tailored to the available financial and human resources.
Psychological climate	The psychological climate in the organization is determined by the interplay of expectations from the MIS, the quality of the MIS, and organizational perceptions of the MIS.
	The information manager should strive to establish a high but realistic level of expectations and to provide high-quality systems.
Nature of the problem	The kinds of problems for which information systems are developed depends on the industry, the level of management involved, the functional area of the organization, and the time frame of the problem.
	The more difficult a problem, the greater the value of a successful solution. Some problems, however, are not amenable to solution by computerized information systems.

Table 2-1 (cont.)

	The MIS manager should distinguish between problems amenable to information-based solutions and those which are not and should reject plans to implement systems when the nature of the problem is inappropriate.
Extraorganizational situation	The extraorganizational situation determines the availability of decision techniques, hardware, software, and personnel. Projects should be tailored to the availability, outside the organization, of those resources which are not available internally.

Notes

1. R.A. Kronenberg, "Weyerhaeuser's Management Information System," *Datamation*, vol. 13, no. 5 (May 1967), pp. 28-30.

2. Howard F. Van Zandt, "How To Negotiate in Japan," *Harvard Business Review*, vol. 48, no. 6 (November-December 1970), pp. 45-56.

3. Jackson Grayson, Jr., "Management Science and Business Practice," *Harvard Business Review*, vol. 51, no. 4 (July-August 1973), pp. 41-48.

4. F. Warren McFarlan, "Problems in Planning the Information System," *Harvard Business Review*, vol. 49, no. 2 (March-April 1971), pp. 74-89.

5. Ibid.

6. Henry C. Lucas, Jr. *Why Information Systems Fail*. New York: Columbia University Press, 1974; see also Lucas "Performance and the Use of an Information System," *Management Science*, vol. 21, no. 8 (April 1975), pp. 908-919.

7. Harlan D. Mills, *Mathematics and the Managerial Imagination* (Princeton, N.J.: Mathematica, 1959).

8. Jerome H. Grossman, "Management Information Systems in Medicine," *Sloan Management Review*, vol. 13, no. 2 (Winter 1972), pp. 1-7.

9. Stanley J. PoKempner, "Management Information Systems—A Pragmatic Survey," *The Conference Board Record,* vol. 10, no. 5 (May 1973), pp. 49-54.

10. Grossman, "Management Information Systems in Medicine."

11. Mills, *Mathematics*.

12. H. Igor Ansoff, "Making Effective Use of Computers in Managerial Decision Making." *Automation* (October 1967), pp. 68-73.

13. Rodney H. Brady, "Computers in Top-Level Decision Making." *Harvard Business Review*, vol. 45, no. 4 (July-August 1967), pp. 67-76.

14. Robert G. Murdick and Joel E. Ross, "Future Management Information Systems," parts 1 and 2, *Journal of Systems Management*, vol. 23, nos. 4 and 5 (April and May 1972), pp. 22-25, 32-35.

15. McFarlan, "Problems in Planning the Information System."

Suggested Readings

Grayson, C. Jackson, Jr. "Management Science and Business Practice." *Harvard Business Review* (July-August 1973), pp. 41-48.

Hammond, John. "The Roles of the Manager and Management Scientist in Successful Implementation." *Sloan Management Review*, vol. 15, no. 2 (Winter 1974), pp. 1-24.

Lucas, Henry C., Jr. "Performance and the Use of an Information System." *Management Science*, vol. 21, no. 8 (April 1975), pp. 908-919.

McFarlan, F. Warren. "Problems in Planning the Information System." *Harvard Business Review,* vol. 49, no. 2 (March-April 1971), pp. 74-89.

PoKempner, Stanley J. "Management Information Systems—A Pragmatic Survey." *The Conference Board Record*, vol. 10, no. 5 (May 1973), pp. 49-54.

West, G.M. "MIS in Small Companies." *Journal of Systems Management*, vol. 26, no. 4 (April 1975), pp. 10-13.

3 The MIS Target

In chapter 2 we discussed those factors external to the MIS which may affect its implementation or operation. In this chapter, we assume that top management in the organization has decided to implement management information systems; it is now irrelevant whether the decision was based on a thorough analysis, pragmatic considerations, or merely a legitimization of a situation that evolved fortuitously. After this decision, a process of definition, planning, implementation, evaluation, and modification occurs. Its success depends to a considerable extent on the degree to which it is formalized.

This chapter is devoted to the basis of MIS formalization, particularly the delineation of the MIS target. The MIS target is the organization's definition of its overall approach to the development of management information systems and their purposes, the determination of the priority scheme for developing specific modules or systems, the assignment of goals to each of these systems, and the form in which the preceding elements are documented.

Recall our definition of MIS: a management information system may stand alone, it can be loosely integrated with other management information systems, or it may be an integral module of the MIS. The definition of the MIS target should clarify, in addition to the more specific issues mentioned above, which approach is to be taken.

Defining the MIS target is critical to MIS management. A well-defined MIS target forms a framework within which systems develop and provide criteria for eventual evaluation. Without such definition, systems may evolve that are inconsistent with one or more elements of the total structure; also, there is no way to evaluate, after the event, whether the system built is that which was actually intended.

The elements of the definition of an MIS target are discussed in a sequence in which the levels of abstraction and aggregation decline and the levels of detail and operationalization increase. This sequence is exhibited graphically in figure 3-1 and follows the target definition process from initial and general ideas to final specification.

Development Strategy

An organization embarking on MIS development should have a conscious and agreed on development strategy. Although development strategies can

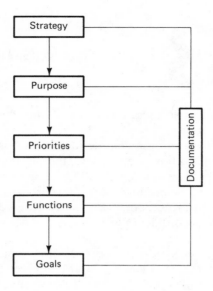

Figure 3-1. Phases of MIS Target Definition

vary widely, the final choice should be the product of overt decisions and not of delegation by default to lower levels in the organization. The organizational development strategy for MIS is a statement of philosophy as much as a guide to the overall approach to implementing management information systems. The strategy is defined along three dimensions:

1. The direction of attack, which determines the degree of comprehensiveness of the development plan
2. The degree of integration, which specifies how much integration is planned among the various management information systems in the organization
3. The propensity to pioneer, which sets the degree of innovativeness desired in MIS development

These dimensions are not independent. A decision to copy successful implementations while foregoing innovation may dictate loosely integrated systems and a low level of comprehensiveness. On the other hand, a decision to develop a comprehensive model of the organization as perceived by top management may require full integration of subsystems and a high degree of innovation.

Direction of Attack

This dimension of the development strategy expresses the basic philosophy of the organization toward MIS development efforts. Several such philosophies, each quite distinct, are spread along a continuum from completely comprehensive to highly modularized in terms of organizational subsystems. The direction of attack is just as important an element of MIS strategy as it is of military strategy; in military strategy the reference is to geographical direction related to the topographical structure of the theater of operations, whereas in MIS it is a conceptual direction related to the hierarchical and functional structure of the organization.

There is a distinct analogy between the direction of attack in MIS development and approaches to organizational growth in general. Growth may be centrally planned within top management so that each element (products, markets, production capacity, and manpower development) is interwoven in the general plan; on the other hand, units of the organization may be encouraged to introduce and implement new projects related to growth. A mixture of these approaches is usually adopted, providing a specific level of comprehensiveness. The direction of attack for MIS development may be considered in similar terms.

In decreasing order of comprehensiveness and increasing order of modularity, the directions of attack for MIS development are (1) top-down, (2) inside-out, (3) parallel or feedback, (4) bottom-up, and (5) evolutionary or modular. While reading the discussion of these approaches, think of types of organizations or organizational situations in which each may be most appropriate. The discussion itself does not follow this order, but instead deals with the approaches in a sequence which highlights their main elements.

Top-down versus bottom-up. In a *top-down* direction of attack, the information needs of management are first specified within an overall model of the organization; the system is then designed to meet those needs. At the opposite end of the spectrum is the *bottom-up* approach, in which operations modules are designed and built within some general conceptual framework and then successively integrated into MIS.

It is undoubtedly significant that the top-down approach is generally favored by academics while practitioners incline to the bottom-up approach. For example, Zani advocates the top-down approach because he feels it is the best way to focus on key tasks and decisions in the organization and then to develop MIS to support these tasks and decisions.[1] Because he attributes great importance to weaving the MIS into the strategy of the organization, he stresses the necessity that MIS be initiated at a high conceptual level as well as at a high level of management. Proponents of this approach tend to be derogatory about the bottom-up approach and refer to it as "a crazy quilt of residues" or "corporate modeling as an afterthought." These remarks highlight their feeling that MIS development should be a conscious and central mission of the organization.

The arguments favoring the bottom-up approach tend to be pragmatic rather than ideological: their major defense is that it works. In practice, most effective MIS efforts seem to be based on a bottom-up strategy. The practical advantages of this approach are perhaps exhibited to greatest advantage by its most extreme *evolutionary* or *modular* form. In this strategy, not only is the model of the organization dispensed with, but even the general framework remains undefined. Systems are not only developed on the basis of operational needs but also integrated as needs arise. The nature of the evolution is twofold; first, specific subsystems and modules that are incorporated in MIS evolve over time in response to changing operational needs and to the changing nature of the MIS themselves, which also evolve in accordance with the changing nature and needs of the organization.

"Evolutionary" is a very appropriate description of the bottom-up strategy because it parallels the evolutionary process of biological species adapting to changes in their environments.

The vehemence of the argument between top-downers and bottom-uppers reminds us of the ideological battles reported to Gulliver in Lilliput between Big-Endians and Little-Endians:

It is allowed on all hands, that the primitive way of breaking eggs before we eat them, was upon the larger end: but his present Majesty's grand-father, while he was a boy, going to eat an egg, and breaking it according to the ancient practice, happened to cut one of his fingers. Whereupon the emperor his father, published an edict, commanding all his subjects, upon great penalties, to break the smaller end of their eggs. The people so highly resented this law, that our histories tell us, there have been six rebellions raised on that account. . . Many hundred large volumes have been published upon this controversy: but the books of the Big-Endians have been long forbidden, and the whole party rendered incapable by law of holding employments.[2]

To carry this fanciful analogy to its logical conclusion, we might point to the similarity between the little end of an egg and the top of the organizational pyramid, and between the big end of an egg and the bottom levels of the pyramid. Thus the Big-Endians are the predecessors of the bottom-uppers, and the Little-Endians of top-downers. In Lilliput, the Little-Endians won after a protracted conflict with great losses on both sides.

So confused is this disagreement between top-downers and bottom-uppers that not even the basic characteristics of the two approaches are agreed on. Thus the top-down approach is often denounced by its detractors because of its grandiose aspirations, long development times, and amount of resources required. Others, however, argue that the top-down approach is simple, quick, and less expensive. Because a system designed and implemented top-down will be used initially by top management, rather than at lower echelons of management, its level of aggregation should be high, while the levels of detail and precision may be kept low at this stage without detracting from the usefulness of the system. In later stages, variables may be disaggregated and subsystems added. Hammond views such a system as a "broad-brush picture seen from the top of the company."[3] This picture includes environmental variables as well as indices of organizational operations.

Despite the image of a top-down-bottom-up controversy, these two strategies are by no means mutually exclusive. An organization may build planning and control systems for top management from the top down while *simultaneously* developing operational and operational control systems from the bottom up. This is yet another direction of attack, which may be called *parallel* or *feedback*. In this approach, operational systems and top management systems are developed in parallel, and successively stronger feedback loops established between them. The rationale behind this approach is that most data in top management systems are external to the organization anyway and relate to issues such as trends in the economy, market shares, product cycles, and consumer demand. Thus even if all operations systems in an organization are computerized, they can provide only a small proportion of the total data base required for all MIS, and only aggregate data are required of such systems. Thus there is little point in delaying the development of top management systems for the extended time spans required for completing operations systems. At the same time, there are usually daily operating problems that can be solved by computerization, and it would not make sense to delay their solution until the top-down approach works its way down to their level.

In the first stages of the parallel approach, operations and management systems are conceived, developed, and operated independently. As both types of systems evolve, however, efforts are made to extract as much information as possible from operations systems as input to management systems. At the same time, management systems are built to utilize the information available in those operations systems which have been built. When this approach is followed consistently, the two types of systems will "grow" toward one another and will eventually become integrated into a total corporate information system. This approach will attain the goal of a total corporate system more quickly and with greater incidental benefits along the way than either unidirectional approach.

Another direction of attack is the *inside-out* approach advocated by Hayes and Nolan.[4] This is essentially an evolutionary variant of the top-down approach with overtones of the parallel strategy. They define it as a reconciliation of the "requirements of the computer modeling process with those of the corporate planning process." Thus the computer is exploited, as the opportunity arises, as part of the organizational planning process, such systems later being integrated with other functions.

The significance of the inside-out approach is best illustrated by a typical example described by its proponents. A young MBA, newly appointed to a high managerial position in a corporate division, used the time-sharing service available in the organization to automate preparation of the divisional budget spread sheet. Based on this application, two directions of development were pursued: first, other divisions adopted the model, and second, additions were made to it to incorporate new features. Such an approach may result in duplicating noncomputerized activities without taking into account the possibilities opened up by the new facility. Thus it may result in a repetition of the early development of computerized systems, which tended to automate existing procedures rather than redesigning the procedure to fully exploit the new technology. On the other hand, such an approach promises that the user-designer genuinely wants the system and will use it.

To introduce some rationality into the ideologically charged competition between the different directions of attack, as at so many other points in this text, we feel the solution should be sought on a contingency basis. The best strategy for an organization is at least partly contingent on its structure and on the kinds of problems with which it is faced. Each strategy may provide a successful solution when applied in the appropriate circumstances.

The top-down approach is well suited to organizations that are characterized by a high degree of centralization, rigid hierarchy, standard operating procedures, and slowly changing environment and overall tasks. The top-down approach is also useful in a situation in which a system is useless unless built in it entirely. The military and police forces are extreme samples of organizational environments conducive to a top-down strategy, and military command and control systems are good examples of the kind of task to which this approach is particularly appropriate. On the other hand, loosely controlled organizations and tasks in which small subsystems can provide large benefits are the kinds of backgrounds in which the bottom-up approach can be expected to succeed.

The bottom-up strategy is so common and relatively successful because it does not require close association with top management. The top-down approach clearly requires close involvement of top management in the development process; if such involvement is not forthcoming, and frequently it is not, then the likelihood of success is considerably diminished. In the bottom-up approach, top management is neither involved in the initiation and design of each project, nor is it able to direct the general plan that grows out of this form of attack. This factor is cited by proponents of top-down as one of the disadvantages of bottom-up; but if top management is unwilling or unable to become involved, it may permit systems to develop without them. In such circumstances, different interest groups—manager-users as well as implementors—compete for information system resources. Top management then decides on resource allocation rather than on the specifics of projects and so is released from intimate involvement.

The evolutionary approach is successful when the organization is not yet ready for sophisticated systems and needs to evolve itself. Thus information systems should evolve together with the organization as it becomes more receptive to them. This strategy is optimal when systems are supposed to cross the lines of organization subsystems or when it is necessary to provide individual modules on a crash basis for specific needs. This strategy is also reasonable for an organization embarking on information system development for the first time because it allows for the evolutionary adaptation of the hardware, software, and manpower elements of this new function in the organization.

Degree of Integration

The second dimension of the development strategy is the degree of integration planned for management information systems in the organization. Integration in information systems is generally considered desirable for several reasons. The more integrated information systems are, the less redundancy appears in the data and the higher the level of consistency of the data used at different places in the organization; the higher the level of integration the easier it is to produce outputs referring to several aspects of the organization and thus the more readily can reports be produced that are useful to higher echelons in the organization; finally, the higher the level of integration, the more accurately the realities of the situation are reflected in the picture of the organization contained in the data base.

On the other hand, many practical difficulties connected with information system integration must be weighed against these advantages. First, the technological complexity of highly integrated systems requires sophisticated hardware and software and therefore complicates project development and operation. This technological complexity leads naturally to high costs, which in turn limit the profitability of highly integrated systems. Furthermore, doubts have been raised about the conceptual ability of managers to grasp the intricacies of highly integrated systems; thus the bounds of cognitive rationality may severely limit the ability to construct highly complex systems.

A further impediment arises from the nature of MIS and their role in the organization. An integrated MIS, by definition, crosses the borders of organizational units. It cuts across functional boundaries, divisional lines, and hierarchical levels. Thus, an integrated MIS should not be under the jurisdiction of any one of the managers whose units supply its inputs or use its outputs. Furthermore, as a result of the rationalization inherent in MIS design, the design and implementation processes often change, or at least tend to call for change, in the jurisdictions of managers. Thus problems of organizational politics are added to the list of more objective problems.

Each organization has its own particular level of integration between its components. Some organizations are monolithic and run directly by top management all the way down to routine, day-to-day problems. Other organizations are loose federations of largely independent suborganizations in which top management restricts itself to general policy, long-range direction, and overall resource allocation. Each form of organization requires a different degree of MIS integration, one that is commensurate with its corporate personality. The wider and more diversified the range of organizational activities, the looser the integration must be.

MIS, however, should not be considered as playing a purely adaptive role in centralization and decentralization. Over the last fifteen years, changes have been recorded in the degree of centralization of organizations. Organizations that decentralized in the forties and fifties have since reverted to higher degrees of centralization. This reversal must be attributed, at least in part, to the developments in information-processing technologies that made it feasible for top management to increase its role and deepen its control of large diversified organizations. Thus increased centralization has been observed among firms using computer systems for some time and, conversely, these firms exhibit a trend toward increasing use of integrated systems. This tendency, caused in part by computer economics favoring large centralized computer systems, may be halted by the introduction of minicomputers. Some authorities predict that the widespread use of minis may prevent the drift towards greater integration in MIS and so in the host organization as well.[5] Thus organizational centralization and information system integration are closely related and should be mutually determined.

Just as the organization is required to make a strategic decision concerning its direction of attack, so must it decide where it wishes to be on the continuum between total integration and total modularity (one might facetiously say "disintegration"). These two aspects of strategy formulation are deliberately treated in conjunction because they are closely connected. On the one hand, a top-down direction of attack leads naturally to a higher level of integration than the bottom-up approach. Furthermore, those features of organizations which are conducive to a top-down approach are also sympathetic to high levels of integration. Because these two decisions complement one another, they must be consistent and should be considered together within the context of the nature of the organization. The organization, the direction of attack, and the degree of information system integration must be mutually consistent and collectively adaptive.

Readiness to Pioneer

The third dimension of the MIS development strategy is the organization's determination of its readiness to play a pioneering role in MIS development. During MIS development, an organization may break new ground in hardware, software, or management technologies. In extreme cases, a firm may have to pioneer in all three areas.

Hardware is the area in which trailblazing is most conspicuous, although probably not most common. Examples of hardware innovation are the first business application of computers by General Electric for payroll computation in 1951, the development of magnetic ink recording and reading by the banking industry for check clearing, the development of special terminals for airline ticket booking, electronic reading of railroad freight car identification, and the current pioneering applications of human voice input.

Most such innovations are implemented at the operations level to permit more efficient operations. The data made available in this manner, however, often spill over into management systems. Thus the immediate availability of data on airline bookings or freight car location permits improved scheduling and better data for long-range planning. There are few examples of hardware technology impacting directly on MIS, apart perhaps from the low-speed terminal (keyboard and character printer or CRT) that permits managers to interface with systems directly rather than necessitating the intervention of computer operators. We predict that the next technological breakthrough that directly affects MIS will be the widespread use of voice inputs, permitting managers to address systems verbally. The importance of such a development is discussed in chapter 9.

MIS pioneering is most frequently evident in the area of system and application programs. Data-base management systems and communications and inquiry systems are examples of the kinds of general purpose, or systems, software in which organizations may find the technologies in common use to be insufficient and so may have to open up new avenues in the course of MIS development. Especially common is the need to develop new applications programs—programs tailored to the specific nature and needs of the organization. If a firm is the first in its industry to develop an MIS, or if it is the first to do so in a particular area of application, it will inevitably have to pioneer in its particular area. This is by far the most widespread form of pioneering and that to which the term is usually applied.

The third type of innovation in management technology is the use of new techniques for decision making or the use of established techniques in new areas. For example, linear programming, which was developed some thirty years ago, has since been gradually applied in many areas such as oil refining, agricultural crop planning, livestock feed mix, and bank resource allocation. In each area, some firm pioneered the use of the new decision technique in its field. The use of statistical forecasting methods is another example of the introduction of new management techniques into MIS in recent years.

The degree of innovation must depend on the organizational situation. Successful innovation depends, above all, on the availability of competent personnel who are able to master new technologies and develop new systems without a model to copy. These circumstances invariably give rise to unforeseen problems that may require considerable resourcefulness for their solution.

Pioneering new systems is a very high-risk activity in which success is by no means guaranteed. This being the case, even greater care should be taken in evaluating such systems than is required with more conventional systems.

Because of these difficulties, firms often tend to hang back and wait for others to incur the costs of innovation. A number of reasons, however, motivate firms to innovate, despite the risks involved, such as the competitive advantages that may accrue from being first in the field with an advanced system, an urgent problem that cannot await other organization's innovations, or an organization so unique that no other organizations are likely to produce models which could profitably be emulated. The last cause is especially powerful.

A major reason for firms to develop their own systems, rather than adopting program packages, is that each organization is sufficiently unique so that prefabricated packages are rarely satisfactory in anything but highly standardized situations. This argument becomes more cogent the higher the level of management to be served. Though some operations may often be sufficiently standardized to adopt readymade packages, more often at higher levels of management different organizational philosophies, structures, and styles of management dictate individually tailored systems. In conclusion, each organization must carefully examine its situation to determine the degree of innovation best suited to its needs.

The Purpose

The purpose of an MIS is a concise, explicit statement of the role assigned a particular information system in the organization. It is required to focus planning and implementation efforts. Hayes and Nolan cite the case of a large organization that embarked on an impressive program of MIS development.[6] A development team, including qualified planners, management scientists, and MBAs was assembled. Top management participated in such major decisions as the data to be collected, the level of aggregation, choice of optimization or simulation techniques, and choice of deterministic or stochastic approaches. No decision, however, was made about the purpose of the system and its intended use was not stated specifically. After four years of development effort, the organization was merged with another. Work on the project was terminated. The MIS failure in this case could be attributed to many factors, but one fact stands out; for four years, large amounts of the resources of the organization were invested in a project whose purpose was never defined.

Four different purposes of MIS have been identified. In order of frequency of occurrence, the purposes assigned to MIS are:

1. A decision aid
2. A planning tool, in the form of an analog, or model, of the organization
3. An information bank
4. A problem identification aid

Clearly, these four purposes overlap considerably and any MIS contains elements of each. Successful MIS programs, however, are distinguished inter alia by being focused on a single predominant purpose.

A Decision Aid

Defined as decision aids, MIS may be found serving all levels of management. At the lower levels, MIS assist in routine decision making, while at higher levels they serve such important, nonrecurring decisions as the introduction of new products, overseas investments, acquisitions, and divestments. Such systems provide analytical and statistical tools to help managers implement explicit decision processes employing scientific methodology. Typically, each decision problem requires a specific type of analysis of the relevant data, which also change from one problem to the next. MIS of this type provide a variety of analytic techniques for data inputs, which are not predetermined.

A Planning Tool or Model

When systems are generalized to encompass most of the major decisions of the organization and to project their effects for a number of years into the future, they become tools for organizational planning, especially if they are designed to simulate the organization, or major portions of it, to answer questions of the "what if" type. "What will be the effect on profits of an overseas investment if the rate of exchange rises 10 percent?" "What will be the contribution to cash flow of the new product if our market share is 15 percent?'' Such systems are generally financially oriented to project the effects of possible decisions on the financial reports. Because planning is an ongoing, iterative process, planning MIS are also generally designed for repetitive use, with fairly well-defined and unchanging input data forms.

An Information Bank

An MIS of this type is designed to store as much relevant information for the organization as feasible—for example, legal precedent information systems and military intelligence systems. In such systems, precise information and processing needs are not specified in advance because they are unknown; only as specific contingencies develop do the needs of the managers become clear. Thus systems of this type are encyclopedic; their construction emphasizes providing a flexible query language, so that virtually any question can be formulated unambiguously; structuring the data base, so that most conceivable questions can be answered within a reasonable time; and providing for constant update of the data in the store.

A Problem-Finding Aid

Before problem solving and decision making take place, the problem or decision situation must first be recognized. Simon views problem identification as an integral and important part of the manager's responsibility.[7] MIS, then, may be defined as a tool for pointing out existing and potential problems. In fact, one of the first steps of electronic data processing in the direction of MIS was the development of the concept of "management by exception"—the recognition that managers do not need all the details of everything that is happening in the organization and that their work can be made much more efficient by bringing to their attention only those cases which indicate the existence of, or potential for, deviation from the acceptable. Thus management by exception is clearly a rudimentary form of problem identification. The concept of problem recognition may be generalized to encompass decision situations in general, and then it includes the identification of opportunities as well as of problems. The latter system is a more advanced type because it requires much external information, whereas problem identification relies mainly on data internal to the organization.

As we pointed out at the beginning of this section, organizations that are successful in MIS development usually single out one of the four purposes as being of overriding interest. Furthermore, there is a relationship between the purposes chosen for MIS in an organization and its development strategy. A modular strategy lends itself most naturally to the development of problem-finding aids within the modules and to the development of information banks. The first step towards integration of systems developed under a modular strategy is often the collection of data from the modules into a central data bank. A more comprehensive approach, on the other hand, encourages modeling and the development of decision and planning aids. Thus the definition of the development strategy and the purpose should be mutually consistent; it clearly does not make sense to consider the construction of a model of the organization within the framework of a modular, bottom-up strategy. Nor is a top-down approach consistent with the development of detailed data banks. Thus an explicit statement of the purpose of the MIS is essential to provide an overall sense of direction to MIS development and to ensure the internal consistency of the development program.

Priorities

Every organization has an enormous number of potential MIS projects. The availability of resources—both human and financial—are the constraints that make it impossible to implement all potential projects simultaneously and force choice between projects. Whether the organization is conducting initial experiments with MIS or whether it is considering additions and modifications to mature systems, it should set criteria for initiating and choosing projects for implementation. The product of these criteria is a priority scheme that determines the sequence of project implementation. The importance of such a scheme is indicated by a number of reports that attribute MIS failures to problems with priorities.

An appropriate priority scheme issues from the development strategy and purpose, which in turn are derived from the objectives of the organization and should be compatible with them. Once the purpose has been defined, proposed projects will contribute in different measures to its attainment, and their priorities should be rated accordingly. For example, computerization of transactions systems may be the basis for a problem identification system, but only of marginal value in building a model of the organization. A simulation model of part of the organization may be an important module in a model of the organization or for the development of a problem-solving aid, but of little use in constructing an information bank.

In addition, priorities should be consistent with the development strategy. A top-down approach dictates a priority scheme that favors planning-oriented projects to operational or control projects. A modular or evolutionary approach, on the other hand, calls for a reversal of these priorities. In more general terms, the priority scheme has to be geared to the level of management for which MIS are to be developed.

Some organizational priorities cannot be conveyed adequately by the development strategy or the definition of purpose of MIS. These preferences tend to relate to specific facets of the organization rather than to the overall approach. Thus the organization may assign high priority to developing MIS in a specific division because it faces the heaviest competition or is expected to expand rapidly. Or top priority may be assigned some critical function in the organization—perhaps transportation in a fresh produce distribution firm, or procurement in a food-processing plant, or marketing in a retail chain. In periods of growth and diversification, organizations will emphasize projects related to new products, investments, and acquisitions. In periods of consolidation and reorganization, the emphasis will be on formalizing and optimizing existing operations. Thus the priority scheme will derive directly from organizational objectives as well as indirectly from them, via the MIS strategy.

A serious problem in defining the priority scheme is the need to build the right amount of flexibility into it. On the one hand, a highly flexible scheme may allow sudden changes in emphasis creating interruptions, frustrations, and waste of resources. A too rigid scheme, on the other hand, may divorce it from the objectives of the organization as they change. In a volatile environment, the problems and objectives of the organization may change rapidly and the priority scheme should be geared to adjust to such changes as the need arises.

In conclusion, the priority scheme provides the guidelines for choice between potential MIS projects to keep them in line with the mainstream of organizational objectives.

Functions

The functions of an MIS are the specific applications developed for use by managers in the organization. The full range of possible functions is as yet undefined but is clearly enormous because, first, some functions are unique to each branch of the economy and to each individual organization and even to each manager. Second, the list of applications is not static, but evolves as new ideas are born, new opportunities and needs arise, and new management techniques are developed. Thus it is futile to compose a universal list of possible areas of application, which is constantly growing and which must already encompass many thousands of areas. However, both computing and management technology limit the ability to implement systems that imaginative managers can devise; expansion of the areas of application is limited as much, or more, by the constraints in the state of the art of management as it is by constraints in computer hardware or computability.

For example, Schwartz has described the range of possible MIS applications, at ESSO.[8] Information systems at ESSO were classified into six types: operating systems, management systems, planning and control systems, management information systems, business transaction systems, and business environment systems. Over forty subareas were enumerated within the six system areas, including business environment, management, management information, and planning and control systems, at least four of which would appear to fall within our definition of MIS. Within the main areas, the detailed list of specific subareas includes systems related to key issues in the organization such as supply and demand, manpower, budgets, and consolidations; systems related to elements in the environment such as customers, government, stockholders, and manpower markets; and investigation systems such as opportunity identification and evaluation, investment planning and evaluation, and operations control and evaluation. This incomplete list from a single firm gives some idea of the range and scope of possible information system functions.

Functions are identified and included in the list of potential applications by a process that depends on the development strategy, the purpose of MIS, and the feasibility of the applications themselves. The development strategy affects the process by determining the location in the organization at which the process is initiated. A comprehensive or top-down approach tends to create a framework in which projects are initiated and evaluated in a central planning group. Under more modular or bottom-up strategies, proposals for applications tend to originate spontaneously at the locations in which needs arise.

The consideration given proposals for application is affected by the purpose of MIS and the priority scheme derived from the purpose. Because the number of potential applications is so large, attention and resources will be channelled into areas compatible with the purpose of MIS and therefore of high priority. It is useful to think of priority assignment as a two-stage process: first, all infeasible projects are eliminated, because there is little point in assigning priority to a project that cannot be implemented. Second, priorities are assigned to those projects which are feasible. Note that the same criteria, or units of measure, play a part in determining both feasibility and priority. Thus a rate of return above a certain level may be considered necessary for a project to become feasible. Above the minimum, projects are priority-rated according to this same criterion.

The correct assessment of feasibility and assignment of priorities is a critical factor in the success and failure of MIS. Five criteria are used in organizations to evaluate feasibility and assess priorities: (1) direct impact on profitability, (2) indirect impact on profitability, (3) institutional criteria, (4) major problems or key tasks, and (5) organizational sophistication. Though all are intuitively obvious, only the first criterion is at all amenable to quantification and measurement. As a result, establishing feasibility and priorities is not simple and may require considerable intuition to answer such questions as "Which application has higher priority—the one with low direct profitability and high impact on a major problem, or the one with high indirect profitability and low impact on major problems?"

Direct Impact on Profitability

Computers were first used to automate clerical work; little or no change occurred in the procedures themselves. At this stage, the savings in costs were the only benefit attributed to the system and were, furthermore, relatively easy to calculate. As systems became more sophisticated, procedures were improved, leading to additional savings in operations; for example, savings in operations are lower inventories resulting from automated inventory management, more efficient use of facilities with computerized production scheduling, and fewer bad debts by automating collection systems. These savings are more difficult to estimate than straight cost replacement, but, with some effort, reasonable estimates can be made.

The real problem in calculating direct benefits arises when the system generates new revenues rather than brings savings. Thus a system may generate revenues by permitting better order processing, more complete market coverage, or fewer stockouts. Such benefits are extremely difficult to estimate in advance because there is no accurate method of forecasting the effect of a system; even in retrospect it is impossible to isolate the effects of the system from other phenomena affecting revenues at the same time—such as advertising campaigns, competitive activity, or general economic conditions.

Many problems in information system development have been attributed to this difficulty in computing their benefits. On one hand, it leads to a lack of attention to the cost-effectiveness of systems, which leads to the development of systems whose cost is not justified; many times the decision is an act of faith with respect to the system's payout potential rather than the result of hard analysis.

Nearly all surveys find that the great majority of information systems are not profitable. For example, a survey of 150 of the 500 largest corporations found that only one-third of their computer operations were profitable.[9] Clearly, even when the cost-benefit analysis of a proposed system is difficult, spending considerable effort on the analysis is quite warranted because of the prevalence of uneconomical systems.

A last point in evaluating the direct financial benefits is probably clear but deserves repetition: projects should be evaluated in terms of discounted cash flows (or any other comparable capital budgeting technique) and not on the basis of undiscounted benefits accumulated over the years while ignoring the time value of money. Surprisingly, many organizations employ highly sophisticated capital budgeting systems but evaluate information system projects in terms of their nominal impact on profit and loss statements over a number of years.

Indirect Impact on Profitability

If evaluating the direct costs and benefits of information systems is difficult, assessing the indirect effects on profitability is even harder. Such effects include higher sales caused by better service afforded by a computerized system or increased revenue resulting from the more exact pricing an MIS allows. Such benefits typically accrue from improvements in decision making made possible by an MIS, which in turn issue from improved managerial work environments, rapid or real-time response, more accurate information, and more consistency in information used by different units. Because the benefits of MIS are primarily of this type, evaluating such systems is very difficult. The existence of such benefits renders simple cost-benefit or rate-of-return criteria inadequate.

As yet, there are no realistic cost-benefit formulas for MIS. This lack of adequate measuring devices causes the frequent reluctance to embark on sophisticated MIS projects—precisely because it is difficult to justify them in classical capital budgeting terms. It may also explain the surveys that indicate a minority of profitable systems; it may well be that the systems are not cost-effective in conventional terms but are justified by managers' basic intuitive feelings about their indirect benefits.

The remaining criteria for priority determination are even less tangible and less amenable to quantitative estimation. If the preceding two criteria are measured in terms of profitability, which is itself a recognizable quantity, the remaining three criteria are institutional and there is not even a theoretical quantitative measure for them.

Institutional Criteria

Institutional criteria may be expressed as a series of questions. Are proposed applications consistent with the goals of the organization and do they reinforce these objectives? Is the proposed system compatible with the structure of the organization, or will it attempt to impose a highly centralized approach on a highly decentralized organization or the reverse? Does it contribute to an even balance of information system development within the organization or is one unit pushing ahead while others remain far behind? Are the budgetary and human resources required for developing the system available within the organization or does the danger exist that we may bite off more than we can chew?

Major Problems or Key Tasks

We have two seemingly opposite views and recommendations about major problems. On one hand, applications are expected to address the major problems or key tasks confronting the organization. On the other, systems developers are sometimes advised to be opportunistic, to implement with minimum delay, and to score early victories; such advice is sometimes interpreted operationally by attacking trivial problems to get a system working quickly. This practice, far from "scoring early victories," instead tends to generate disappointment and contempt, which make it much more difficult to build significant systems later on. Early victories can be achieved by approaching the major problems of the organization using the right tactics. Instead of a comprehensive frontal attack that will probably result in complex, time-consuming, and problem-prone systems which will be little appreciated, it is advisable to choose a relatively simple subsystem that can make a major contribution within a key problem area. Examples might include a stolen car reporting system for a police department; inpatient laboratory report records for a hospital, delivery route planning for a dairy firm, or cash flow forecasting for a finance company.

Organizational Sophistication

Applications selected must be consistent with the level of sophistication of the organization in general and with its information-processing sophistication in particular. Especially in the early phases of MIS development, an organization will probably not be able to absorb a highly sophisticated system successfully. In the early stages, simple systems based on existing procedures may be most effective; only after some experience has been acquired will it be feasible to contemplate systems requiring significant upgrading of the level of operations in the organization.

Because four of these five criteria are intangibles, obviously ordering priorities is not a technical matter that can be left to experts. Priorities can only be determined by experienced managers relying on their judgment and intuition. Because of this, however, it becomes extremely important that such deliberations be conscious and formalized in the form of reports specifying the reasons for establishing specific priority schemes. Such documents permit subsequent tests for changes in the situation on which the priorities were based and will indicate when the need to update priorities has arisen.

Goals

Each function chosen for implementation has to be assigned specific goals that should reflect priority criteria and that are stated in the same terms; they must also be consistent with the overall purpose chosen for MIS. Thus the goals are a further step toward the operationalization of the general concept embodied in the purpose and are also a first iteration towards defining the specific requirements or specifications of systems. Thus goals play the same role for individual functions as the purpose does for the overall system.

The goals are not exact numerical specifications but rather describe the system generally in order of magnitude and qualitative terms. Thus they provide beacons toward which the system's designers should head and constraints from which they should not stray. They fall into two broad categories—goals describing expected benefits and goals relating to system characteristics.

Benefit Goals

These goals indicate the benefits the organization expects to receive from the system in direct cost savings or increased revenues. Furthermore, because defining benefits without reference to cost is of little value, the budget and manpower goals of the system are an integral part of this phase of system definition. The cost goals need to be especially emphasized because in practice they are often ignored. Actual project costs are often two or three times the initial estimate. Benefits also tend to be overestimated, leading to dangerous deviations of system profitability from plans. The problem of controlling system costs is discussed in chapter 4, but any effective control mechanism must have a clearcut goal to which it can relate.

Intangible benefits expected to originate from the system should also be clearly specified; such as improved service to customers, better corporate planning and control, maintaining technical progress, better market information, and improved product planning. These goals provide yardsticks against which the performance of the future system can be evaluated in just the same way as the tangible benefit goals.

System Characteristics Goals

These goals describe the way the system should operate to achieve the tangible and intangible benefit goals. Such goals relate primarily to information content, response times, and system reliability, although others may be relevant in specific circumstances.

The information content goal defines the kinds of information to be maintained by the system—information about competitors, research projects, or managerial employees. These goals should also specify in general terms such characteristics of the information as level of accuracy, required recency, and degree of security.

The response-time goal indicates the time that may be permitted to elapse between the occurrence of an event in the real world and its reflection as information in the system. For military command or process control systems this time might be measured in seconds. For bank resource allocation or hospital scheduling systems, a response time of one or two days should be quite satisfactory. For a budget planning and control system, a response time of several weeks or perhaps even months may be adequate. Because decreasing response times can be very expensive, the response time goal should be compatible with the purpose and benefits goals but not unnecessarily rigorous.

Finally, the system-reliability goal indicates the allowable failure rates and degree of backup required. Again, different systems have very different kinds of requirements. A space flight control system is planned for zero failure and must have immediate and complete backup. A bank, on the other hand, must have complete backup for data, but can afford to have the system down occasionally for a few hours. Systems working on long-range planning can afford to be down for several days with no damage done. Just as decreasing response times is expensive, so is increasing reliability, and the same criteria of compatibility with purpose and benefits and the same warning against expensive overkill apply.

In conclusion, goal definition is an intermediate stage in system operationalization. It is the first step toward transforming the somewhat nebulous purpose into a concrete system by specifying what the benefits of the system are expected to be—that is, what the system is going to do and what general characteristics are required to realize those benefits.

Documentation

Documentation is a process that should accompany all the previously mentioned phases of defining the MIS target. It is the form in which MIS targets are presented to top management for evaluation and control. The same documentation provides the terms of reference for systems developers as they begin developing system specifications. One of the most significant factors differentiating companies which are effective information system users from those which are not is the quality and content of their written plans. Thus despite its seemingly technical appearance, this is an issue to which management is well advised to address itself.

The problem is that documentation is generally perceived as a dreary chore and a marginal task that may be postponed, delegated to a junior staff member, or generally ignored. However, if documentation of the strategic decisions in MIS development is incomplete or nonexistent, management will later be unable to perform its control function; it will be unable to verify whether it is getting the product it ordered. Furthermore, without adequate documentation, system developers will often have to decide for themselves on issues that should be the prerogative of top management and on which it may have in fact made decisions. In such circumstances, systems developers will make decisions in line with their own perceptions and interests rather than with the needs and wishes of management. Mutual disenchantment is the inevitable result of the lack of common terms of reference, which can only be properly provided by adequate documentation.

Several experts have suggested detailed documentation schemes listing the topics to be covered and the method of their presentation.[10] Though the specific form of the documentation is of no great consequence, completeness of coverage is of primary importance. Basically, all stages of MIS planning and implementation (discussed in chapter 4) should be thoroughly documented as a guide to development, as a measure for control, and as a basis for reevaluation and change.

The main points made in this chapter and their implications for MIS management are summarized in table 3-1.

Table 3-1
Summary of MIS Target Variables

Variables	Conclusions
Development strategy	An organization should have a conscious and agreed-upon development strategy.
	The degree of comprehensiveness of the direction of attack (top-down; inside-out; parallel or feedback; bottom-up; evolutionary or modular) is contingent on the structure of the organization and the kind of problems it faces.
	A top-down approach suits highly centralized organizations that focus on one major mission.

Table 3-1 (cont.)

	The integration of the MIS should parallel the integration of organizational operations (both should be mutually determined).
	An organization should decide on the degree of innovativeness that suits its risk-taking policy.
The purpose	To focus planning and implementation efforts, the purpose of the MIS should be defined either a decision aid, a planning tool, an information bank, or a problem identification aid.
Priorities	The priority scheme provides guidelines for choice among potential MIS⁻ projects. It issues from the development strategy, purpose, and organizational priorities.
Functions	The full range of the specific MIS applications developed for use by managers in the organization is as yet undefined, enormous, and evolving. The formation of potential applications depends on earlier phases of MIS targeting. Evaluations of feasibility and assessment of priorities use five criteria: direct impact on profitability, indirect impact on profitability, institutional criteria, major problems or key tasks, and organizational sophistication.
Goals	Goals assigned to each function reflect the purpose of the MIS and describe the function in order of magnitude and qualitative terms. Goals refer to expected benefits or system characteristics.
Documentation	Documentation should accompany all phases and is the form in which MIS targets are presented management for evaluation and control.

Notes

1. William M. Zani, "Blueprint for MIS," *Harvard Business Review*, vol. 48, no. 6 (November-December 1970), pp. 95-100.

2. Jonathan Swift, *Gulliver's Travels* (London: J. M. Dent, 1944).

3. John S. Hammond, III, "Do's and Dont's of Computer Models for Planning," *Harvard Business Review*, vol. 52, no. 2 (March-April 1974), pp. 110-123.

4. Robert H. Hayes and Richard L. Nolan, "What Kind of Corporate Modeling Functions Best," *Harvard Business Review*, vol. 52, no. 3 (May-June 1974), pp. 102-112.

5. See James C. Emery, *Organizational Planning and Control Systems* (London: Macmillan, 1969) for a theoretical discussion of this problem.

6. Hayes and Nolan, "What Kind of Corporate Modeling Functions Best."

7. Herbert A. Simon, *The New Science of Management Decision*, rev. ed. (Englewood Cliffs, N.J.: Prentice-Hall, 1977).

8. M. K. Schwartz, "MIS Planning," *Datamation*, vol. 16, no. 10 (September 1970), pp. 28-31.

9. Roger Gupta, "Information Manager: His Role In Corporate Management," *Data Management*, vol. 12, no. 7 (July 1974), pp. 26-29.

10. Lists of topics to be documented can be found in F. Warren McFarlan, "Problems in Planning the Information System," *Harvard Business Review*, vol. 49, no. 2 (March-April 1971), pp. 74-89; and Schwartz, "MIS Planning."

Suggested Readings

Ein-Dor, Phillip. "Parallel Strategy for MIS." *Journal of Systems Management*, vol 26, no. 3 (March 1975), pp. 30-35.

Hayes, Robert H., and Nolan, Richard L. "What Kind of Corporate Modeling Functions Best." *Harvard Business Review*, vol. 52, no. 3 (May-June 1974), pp. 102-112.

McFarlan, F. Warren. "Problems in Planning the Information System." *Harvard Business Review*, vol. 49, no. 2 (March-April 1971), pp. 74-89.

Schwartz, M. K. "MIS Planning." *Datamation*, vol. 16, no. 10 (September 1970), pp. 28-31.

Zani, William M. "Blueprint for MIS." *Harvard Business Review*, vol. 48, no. 6 (November-December 1970), pp. 95-100.

4   The MIS Project

Once the environment of an MIS has been analyzed and the MIS target defined, the time is ripe to undertake construction of the system. The MIS project is the mechanism that deciphers the plans embodied in the target definition and translates them into a working system at the disposal of the organization. This chapter discusses the elements of project execution and their application in such a way as to ensure the success of the project.

During this discussion, we often refer to "the MIS"; these references are to the particular MIS being constructed and do not indicate that we have reverted to the concept of a single, total, integrated information system. In practice, several MIS may be under construction at the same time and each should be considered as a separate MIS project for which all of the elements we discuss are relevant. A distinction should be made, however, between a first MIS project, in which manpower and organizational elements will be extremely important, and subsequent projects, in which changes in these elements will tend to be more incremental.

Though this chapter is devoted to the technical and organizational aspects of the MIS project, such projects clearly also have important behavioral aspects. The three groups of participants in the process of developing an MIS—top management, implementors, and users, the relationships between them, and their effects on the process are discussed in separate chapters for the sake of clarity.

Also, the success of an MIS project is not synonymous with success of the MIS itself. We defined a successful MIS as one that is intensively and beneficially used by one or more satisfied managers. The definition of the MIS target is the process whereby such systems are specified within the context of organizational goals, strategies, and needs. The objective of the MIS project is to place the specified system at the disposal of the organization. Thus we define a successful MIS project as one that furnishes the organization, on schedule and within budget, with a system with design specifications that conform to project goals and implementation that meets design specifications. It follows that a successful MIS may be produced by an unsuccessful project—one that was behind schedule or beyond its budget. Conversely, a successful project that provides the specified system on time and within budget may result in an unused and unsuccessful MIS if the specifications are incorrect.

This chapter is divided into four parts. The first part deals with the stages of the MIS project; it begins where the MIS target left off and ends with a routinely running system. The remaining three parts deal with the resources that are incidental to the stages of the project and that comprise the final system—that is, hardware, software, and people. These resources are considered in terms of the acquisition strategies for hardware and software required by the system and the organizational arrangements for its implementation.

The Stages of the MIS Project

The MIS project is a process composed of two stages—technical execution and managerial control. In the basic model each execution stage terminates in an appropriate management control phase. The project can be thought of as a series of cycles, each of which executes one phase of the construction and is completed only after the control phase has approved the execution and given the go-ahead for the next cycle. This concept clearly implies that two distinct kinds of skills are required for executing the MIS project, as for any other complex project; the requisite technical skills must be available to guarantee the skillful performance of the technical phases, and management skills are required to ensure that the control phases are performed and in fact keep the project under control.

The need for effective and timely control cannot be overemphasized. Numerous projects are ineffectively controlled and eventually abandoned many years beyond the planned completion date, with expenditures two or three times the budget allocated. Thus the economic cost of ineffective control can be extremely high and can be aggravated by the mistrust such experiences will tend to generate in the organization. Negative attitudes fertilized by project failures will tend to retard the development of MIS in general, not only of the particular project involved.

The execution phases are exhibited, in chronological sequence, on the left of figure 4-1, whereas the control phases relevant to each execution phase are on the right. Each section that follows discusses one of the phases; special emphasis has been placed on pathologies that have been identified as frequent causes of project failure.

System Specifications

Implementation of an MIS project begins with the MIS target as a framework. The target, however is not sufficiently detailed to be operational as a blueprint for system development. The first stage of the project consists of translating system goals into concrete specifications, including

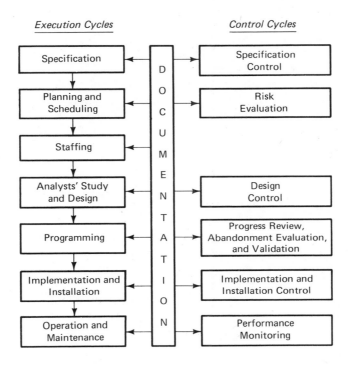

Figure 4-1. Sequence of Execution and Control Cycles in MIS Project Implementation

technical, time-table, and budget specifications for the specific project. At this stage the principal responsibility passes from top management or its delegates who are heavily involved in defining the MIS target to information system management who are responsible for executing and operating the systems outlined in that target. This is why controls become so important at this stage. To this point, executives have been intimately involved in the process; from this point on, project management will be largely independent, except for the controls and reviews instituted by management. If these controls are weak, project management will be virtually free to do as it finds fit. However, even when motivated by the best of intentions, the decisions of project managers are often far from consistent with the objectives of executive management.

Technical Specifications. The technical requirements of an organization determine the specifications of the particular system and place constraints on the project for its development. The quality of these specifications and the degree to which they are consistent with the MIS target affect the success of the MIS (not of the MIS project, but of the MIS itself, as measured by the intensity of use). This topic is discussed in chapter 9. The aspects that directly affect the MIS project are briefly discussed here.

Because projects differ considerably, not all parameters need be specified for all projects. Clearly, however, the more fully a system is specified, the less the probability that mistakes will be made in construction. Following is a list of parameters most frequently specified for MIS projects:

> Quality of information, comprising levels of accuracy, integrity and timeliness

> Input and output characteristics of data, including methods of collection and display

> System operating characteristics include mode of operation (such as batch, on-line, or time sharing) and priority scheduling schemes

> Security and privacy requirements

> System capacity in terms of transactions per hour, input, and output rates

> Time constraints as measured by response times or processing schedules

> System quality, including hardware and software reliability

> User interface requirements including ease of use, flexibility, and capacity for evolution

> Sophisticated information-processing and management-science techniques

For any project, these parameters need to be operationalized and assigned specific values. As examples, response times might be specified as 85 percent of inquiries to receive service within 15 seconds and 100 percent to receive service in 60 seconds; user interface requirements might specify no previous computer experience needed to use the system beyond a 15-minute training session, and ability to alter output formats on three days' notice.

During the specification stage it is important to remember that "normal" parameter values are usually attainable at reasonable cost, but that attempts to achieve values very far beyond these can be very expensive. In the preceding response-time example, an attempt to service 95 percent of inquiries within 15 seconds might cost twice as much as servicing 85 percent within this period. It might be quite easy and cheap to attain 98 percent accuracy of records and it might cost as much again to reach 99 percent.

Those engaged in specification must be aware of the cost curves involved and weigh the cost of any specification against its value to the organization and the real degree of necessity. Why specify 10-second response if 15-second delay is just as acceptable and much cheaper?

Time-Table and Budget Specifications. The time-table and budget specifications are partly determined by the development strategy and partly by the technical specifications. If the development strategy is more comprehensive and based on a top-down approach, it will imply larger projects and perhaps even one overall, total project; a bottom-up approach, on the other hand, will prescribe a number of smaller, more readily workable projects.

The technical specifications affect the time table depending on their rigor; the sooner the system is required and the more exacting the demands made on it, the more expensive it will be. Normally, the more exacting the specifications, the more liberal the time table should be. A combination of tight specifications and a pressing schedule can lead to much higher costs than would a more relaxed schedule with the same technical specifications.

Specification Control. Control at the specification stage primarily involves endorsing the technical specifications once it has been certified that they indeed represent the system that was envisaged in the MIS target goals. Because specifications often must be changed during a project as unforeseen problems arise or as new opportunities are discovered, they should be periodically reviewed and updated by management as the need arises.

Time-table and budget specification control is limited at this stage to the overall budget allocation and project completion date. The operationalization of these gross data is the subject of the next stage—project planning and scheduling.

Planning and Scheduling

Frequent delays and requests for supplementary budgets are more often the rule rather than the exception in MIS projects. MIS projects are just as prone as any other complex developmental projects to faulty planning resulting in delivery postponements and cost overruns. The time table and budget specifications are the major control tools available to management to ensure that the project remains on course until completion.

It is not enough to approve a completion date and total budget, which may be one or two years and several hundred thousand, or even million, dollars in the future. Management should insist on a breakdown of the project into a fairly large number of way stations, each with its scheduled date and budget target; such planning will provide early feedback on whether the project is progressing as envisaged or whether severe schedule and cost over-runs are building up. Cost estimates are frequently overoptimistic and it is often extremely difficult to extract from MIS managers any commitment at all on schedules. Top management should be prepared to exert the full weight of its authority to get concrete commitments.

Projects should be divided into controllable workload, schedule, and budget segments. Each segment should be defined so that one person or a small team can complete it within a limited period—for example, in one to three months. There is no one best way to segment and schedule a project. This planning depends heavily on the quality of the implementation personnel, on the internal logic of the project as seen by the planners, and on the control styles of project management.

Once segmented, the segments of the project and the dependencies between them create a plan and schedule network. Such formal planning techniques as Gantt charts or PERT diagrams are not only beneficial in controlling execution, but also in evaluating the plan itself. These techniques permit the simple estimation and aggregation of the budget and schedule factors for each segment and their comparison to the previously estimated total budget and completion date. They also facilitate changes in the plan necessitated by inconsistencies, changes in priorities, or changes in plan dictated by events during the execution itself.

A plan should include milestones along its critical path, each coming after a number of segments. These milestones are predetermined and project management is required to obtain executive approval to proceed beyond each one. Such milestones ensure periodic review of the project as well as users' needs and implementors' practices by top management and will reveal any significant deviations from the plan. The output of this stage is a detailed plan and schedule for the project.

Risk Evaluation. Project planning establishes the yardsticks necessary for management to maintain control over the project. The plan itself, however, should also be evaluated before release for execution. Control of the plan takes the form of a risk evaluation that determines how realistic the plan is and how sensitive to changes are its underlying assumptions. If it is very sensitive and small deviations in critical segments can build up into large completion delays and cost overruns, then the project is risky and management must decide whether the projected benefits justify the risk. If, on the other hand, the plan is based on conservative estimates and is not sensitive to any but major deviations, then the project is relatively risk-free and can be approved without reservation.

Staffing

The availability of qualified staff is one element of the risk evaluation. The degree to which a plan is realistic for a specific organization naturally depends to a considerable extent on the quality of the implementation staff that will execute it. A project that is reasonably risk-free for a high-quality staff may be extremely risky for a less competent development team.

Staffing is the execution phase that follows planning and is usually performed in parallel with it so that on approval of the plan, execution can begin with little delay. Recruiting and training the implementation staff are discussed in detail in chapter 6; they are mentioned here to stress their implications for the planning stage of the project. If the quality of staff assumed by the plan is unobtainable, it may be necessary to modify the plan or even to abandon it. The almost unbelievable variances in the productivity and quality of work of different people in the same job categories ensure that this issue cannot be taken lightly; above all, one cannot just assume that appropriate staff will somehow materialize when needed.

Analysts' Study and Design

With the budgetary, schedule, and technical specifications in hand, the analysts chosen in the staffing stage can begin detailed system design. Normally they begin with a period of study in which they develop a thorough understanding of the problem and chart relevant information flows in the organization. Next they decide on the formats for the data records to be stored and the structure of the data base in which these records will be incorporated. If some data are already available in other systems, the method of obtaining such data must also be determined.

From the outputs specified in the system specifications and the data from which these outputs are to be produced, it is then possible to describe the data-processing functions that are to be performed and the sequence of their execution. Once it is known what and how data are to be processed, it is possible to decide on hardware capable of meeting the storage and processing needs of the system within the response time in the system specification. A new hardware system may be necessary, or it may be sufficient to add resources to an existing computer, or perhaps only registering a claim on current resources is required.

The designers' responsibility does not terminate with presentation of a complete design, but should extend into the next stage—programming—to ensure that the programs written actually conform to the intentions of the design. (See the section on programming later in this chapter.)

The study and design process we have described seems linear; actually, the design phase is highly iterative and problems arising at any step may require retracing the entire process to find a better solution. For example, at the hardware configuration phase it may become clear that a different data base structure from that chosen could lead to significant savings; in turn, record formats might need to be altered. In extreme cases, it may become evident that the system specifications themselves are infeasible, and it may be necessary to reexamine them and to restate them in view of design problems.

Fine-tuning the design may require considerable repetition. For this reason, it is advisable to first do a rough-cut of the whole system to ensure consistency throughout and then to return and flesh out each phase in detail. It is much easier to make changes on a first approximation of each phase than it is to rewrite a completely detailed design.

Again, the importance of documentation cannot be overstated, especially at this level of detail, where many man-months may be wasted without full documentation explaining what designers have done and why. Furthermore, it is almost impossible to evaluate or change a system that is inadequately documented. Thus, instead of serving it, a poorly documented system can become master of the organization, which has to adapt itself to the system it cannot change, rather than the opposite.

Design Control. Design control is a particularly critical phase because management usually drops out of the picture at this point; for the same reason it is also the phase in which many failures originate. The function of design control is to ensure that the analysts' design in fact conforms to the system specifications—in other words, the system will perform as specified if implemented. Control at this stage requires the ability to bridge between the management concepts behind the specifications and the technicalities incorporated in the system design; it requires the ability to envisage the system design as a live system in its intended and specific organizational context.

In most cases, management simply lacks the technical knowledge necessary for control at this stage. The responsibility for control then devolves by default onto information system management, which often does not understand the use implications of compromises with the specifications that it may approve. Therefore information system management should probably have a broad background of management experience in the organization rather than a narrow technical background; if the MIS manager has organizational experience and has acquired a knowledge of the technology, management may safely assign to him responsibility for design control. The only realistic alternative is to employ a consultant with both the technical knowledge and managerial experience necessary; in most cases it is unrealistic to assume that top management will acquire the requisite technical skills.

Programming

In the programming stage, the analysts' design is translated into a working system, implemented on a specific computer configuration. This stage is noteworthy primarily for the proportion of project resources that it absorbs and for the difficulties encountered in controlling this most expensive stage.

In scheduling terms, programming absorbs about 65 percent to 75 percent of elapsed time from project initiation to completion. In terms of personnel, programming typically accounts for 75 percent to 85 percent of the total man-months invested. In addition to these resources, projects are most likely to go awry and generate cost overruns and schedule slippages at this technical stage. As a participant in a NATO conference on software engineering stated:

Production of large-scale software has become a scare item for management. By reputation it is often an unprofitable morass, costly and unending.[1]

Personnel problems and the lack of a sound theoretical basis for estimating the time and cost elements of large programming projects are often cited as reasons for these difficulties. The estimation problem tends to diminish somewhat as experience is acquired with a particular kind of program. The personnel problem, however, retains its urgency because of the extreme variance in programmer productivity, which is about 25 to 1 between the best and worst programmers.[2] Selecting programmers is discussed in chapter 6; however these productivity figures indicate how ineffective the selection process is.

Several recent techniques have been developed in attempts to control the programming problem, including Structured Programming, Improved Programming Techniques (IPT), and better documentation. It is beyond the scope of this book to cover this subject in any detail and it is our intention at this point simply to heighten the reader's awareness of the problem.[3]

Progress Review, Abandonment Evaluation, and Validation of Programming Projects. Successfully programming a system is largely a problem in managing and controlling programming projects. The principles of controlling programming projects are identical to those for any other project, including the overall system implementation project. The difference is in the high risk of failure, the quantity of resources wasted by failure, and the consequent necessity of extremely rigorous application of the principles of project control.

A rigorous programming project management system can alleviate much of the wastefulness that is experienced by companies with more lax control. Organizations with successful information system programs are characterized, among other things, by the insistence of corporate management on development of control tools that pinpoint problems for their immediate attention. As with the overall information system project, programming subprojects should also be phased between a series of intermediate goals with periodic progress reports; this action forces management to compare progress to plans and to decide explicitly how to deal with deviations. Even organizing the programming group as a profit center should be viewed only as a supplement and not as a substitute for step-by-step controls.

Because cost overruns on programming projects sometimes go as high as five times the estimated cost (three times the estimate is quite common), the need to consider abandoning such projects is evident. If the profitability of a project is established at a given budget level, it is rather unlikely that it will still be profitable at several times the proposed budget. It is a common error to continually defer evaluating the desirability of abandonment or even to ignore it completely; in these cases, organizations press on with implementation, regardless of the cost, until well beyond the point where the project can ever be justified. Phased control can aid in avoiding such problems by indicating the potential for large deviations before they are incurred and before the sunk costs and psychological investment blind those responsible to the validity of abandonment as a viable alternative.

A final problem in controlling programming projects is validating the end product; do the programs perform as intended? The only way to validate programs is to prepare test data to cover as many as possible of the circumstances that the programs may encounter. Ignoring validation can lead to a system going down, because of bugs, after the organization has cut over to it and is no longer anchored to a backup system. Programmers in general tend to be somewhat less than completely thorough at this stage; management, with the help of potential users, must verify that the system is as close to complete as they can. The continued involvement of analysts in program control can also help keep programs consistent with the full detail of the system design. Though bugs will inevitably pop up in running programs, their number should be kept to a minimum.

Implementation and Installation

With programming completed and a set of working programs in hand, the system enters the stage of implementation and installation, in which it is started up and run in. This stage consists of entering the initial data with which the system is primed, establishing the routines for feeding update data into the system, and shaking out any remaining bugs discovered only after the system goes onstream. Thus, in a sense, this stage is also a continuation of the program validation stage, in which actual use is a final test on the validity and viability of the programs.

Because unforeseen problems are frequently discovered at this stage and additional time may be required before the system becomes completely operational, it is customary, when an old system is being replaced by the new, to run both systems in parallel until the new system has been thoroughly checked. Obviously, a completely new system should be validated before the developers are released and before it becomes a basis for decision making.

This stage of development brings several new groups of people in the organization into contact with the system and changes the form of contact of others. First, its users, some of whom may have been previously involved in specifying the system, now need to learn how to use it. The personnel who prepare input data for the system will often be required to modify or change their procedures; again a learning process is required. Finally, those responsible for controlling the quality of the input data and of the outputs will also require appropriate training. Thus many people in different capacities need to be trained in new system functions. Success or failure may depend on the quality of such training, because if the personnel do not fully understand their duties, the system cannot function well. Successful implementations are invariably accompanied by well-planned and executed training programs.

Implementation and Installation Control. The main control problem in this stage is to ensure that data flows into and out of the system meet the planned schedule and that the quality of these flows is as specified. In addition, final validation of the system is performed in this stage. These controls are essentially final checks before signing off the implementors and handing over the system to those responsible for its subsequent operation.

At this level, top management must ensure that users are satisfied with the system and that it is operating smoothly before the implementors are relieved of their responsibility. Most of the interactions at this stage will be between MIS management and operating management concerning data flows, on the one hand, and between MIS management and users concerning final adjustments to the system, on the other hand. At the end of this stage, the development project is complete. The remaining stages discussed below are included here to cover the system's entire life-cycle.

Operation, Support, and Maintenance

On completion of the development project, the system enters a period of routine operations. Controls at this stage will center on routine quality control of inputs and outputs on one hand and control of computer center efficiencies on the other.

Quality control of inputs is necessary to ensure that the data input to the system remains within acceptable limits and does not deteriorate as personnel or procedures change. This step is essential to prevent contamination of the data base by faulty data, which may be very difficult to correct later. Quality control of outputs is one way of controlling inputs, because input quality is invariably reflected in the accuracy of outputs. This control is also necessary to maintain users' trust in the system and to prevent the generation of unfavorable attitudes arising from low-quality output.

After a system has been in operation for some time and has stabilized, usually costs can be cut by fine-tuning the system and altering programs to minimize processing times. This control also ensures that the computer is operated efficiently; it avoids wasting time in such sloppy operating procedures as waiting for tape files from the library and inefficient job queuing. The controls at this stage are designed to achieve maximum throughput from the hardware system with the programs available.

By the time a new system is completely operational and debugged, it already lags behind developments in the organization and its environment. The long lead times for system development, changes in top level personnel, and changes in the size, scope, goals, and domains of the organization all dictate changes in information systems. The support and maintenance phase must keep the system as current as possible by updating it when the need arises and also eliminate any remaining errors after extended periods of operation as rare situations are encountered.

The ongoing operation and maintenance of the system should be accompanied by periodic evaluations to determine the need for revisions, especially to determine when the system has been patched so often that it becomes preferable to redesign it rather than putting new patches over the old. Thus the controls in this stage consist of monitoring the performance of the system to update it and to indicate when the life of the current version is drawing to its close and a new life cycle should be initiated.[4]

Documentation

The importance of thorough and accurate documentation is virtually impossible to stress too much. The importance of documentation probably reaches its pinnacle in the project development stage. Because of the number of people who may be involved, the only effective way to coordinate them is in writing.

The need for complete documentation is increased by the rapid turnover often experienced among information system personnel. If such personnel leave without leaving adequate records behind, any work they may have done will become useless and wasted.

Good documentation is also imperative in debugging and updating programs, as described in the operation, support, and maintenance stage. When programs are not properly documented, such changes can be difficult or even impossible and always expensive. All management personnel, both inside and outside the information system function, must constantly ensure that critical documentation standards are maintained.[5]

Equipment Strategy

Information systems can only be programmed for specific hardware configurations; the configuration must be known by the analysts' design phase of the development process because many technical decisions from that point on will be affected by the computer selected. The equipment strategy of an organization relates to the determination of computer capabilities required, the process by which the equipment is selected, the form of acquisition, and the deployment of computer equipment.

Determination of Computer Capabilities

The trade-off between computer capacity and cost is the major problem in determining computer capabilities. On one hand, organizations do not want to spend more on computer hardware than is necessary; on the other, running out of capacity leads to delays in project development and a deterioration in service from existing systems. Although the frequency of trading up equipment has not been related to success, lack of capacity and frequent equipment changes can cause difficulties, which are aggravated because computer configurations are fixed in the short run and are difficult and expensive to change quickly.

Two rules can help to alleviate the constraints of computer capacity. First, initial configurations should be designed with liberal reserve capacity because machine specifications often are insufficient when installed. Second, think in terms of the compatible lines of equipment offered by manufacturers rather than in terms of a single machine; considerable weight should be assigned to upward compatibility and a product line should be chosen that will guarantee relatively simple growth for a number of years without major system changes.[6]

Computer System Selection

The size of the investment in computers, the apparent measurability of computer characteristics, and the expertise involved in their selection have imbued the selection process with an aura of importance similar to that of selecting an expensive stereo system for the home:

There are . . . cases where . . . we feel preoccupation with equipment decisions appears to have impeded progress, by diverting attention from other areas that really determine success.[7]

In the early years of computing, this preoccupation was encouraged by fears that manufacturers were overstating system capabilities and that machines would not perform to specification. Because these fears are no longer valid, there is no reason for investing heavily in system selection. Initial systems should be evaluated on the basis of competitive bids from a number of vendors. Proposals should be scored on cost versus performance, software availability, growth potential, and manufacturer service and support; the scores should be weighted by organizational priorities.[8] The incremental benefits from refining the selection method are slight and lead to long and costly selection procedures that have little real effect on system success.

Form of Acquisition

The basic alternatives are between in-house use (of rented or purchased equipment) and the employment of service bureaus. In-house use provides autonomous control of the hardware facility and eliminates the dependence implicit in the use of service bureau facilities. Thus, on the face of it, in-house installation may appear preferable; none of the field surveys, however, find any connection between the form of acquisition and the success of the system. Thus using a service bureau should be decided on purely economic grounds.

Service bureaus are usually employed by small organizations that cannot afford in-house computing or by organizations in the early stages of information system development that do not yet have sufficient volume to justify their own hardware. With the advent of minicomputers and their revolutionary impact on price and performance, the threshold for in-house computing has dropped so low that all except the smallest businesses will probably have in-house installations. Service bureaus will still have a place, however, both for these small organizations and for handling peak loads for organizations with their own equipment, for providing continuity and flexibility in system upgrading, and for providing specialized services that would be uneconomic in-house.

Equipment Deployment

Equipment deployment is yet another variation of the centralization versus decentralization issue that was discussed in chapters 2 and 3. In this case, the degree of centralization of computer hardware becomes an issue when computer use in an organization expands to the point where more than one computer is required; should all the equipment then be centralized in one location or distributed through the organization? The possibility of organizing minicomputers in networks reduces the threshold at which decentralization becomes possible to a very low level, even in quite small firms.

The continuum of organizational possibilities for hardware location passes through three main points:

1. A large centralized processing complex, probably located at the headquarters of the organization
2. A number of medium to large processors at regional locations
3. Distributed minicomputer networks

Most organizations now regionalize their data-processing capacity rather than centralize or distribute it between users. For example, Ford Motor Company pools computer facilities into centers as large as are consistent with good service.[9] Recently, however, the tendency to disperse computing power has noticeably increased; the Securities and Government Services Group of First National City Bank of New York has shifted from a centralized site with one large computer to a network of eight minicomputers distributed throughout the organization.[10]

Because the same arguments of economy, flexibility, and complexity are made for and against each system, the literature is of little help on this issue. We do expect, however, to see a considerable increase in distributed minicomputer networks, either as stand-alone systems or in support of large central processing facilities. We again offer our golden rule: computing equipment should be located in a manner that is most consistent with the structure, philosophy, problems, and needs of each organization.

Software Strategy

The distinction between hardware and software strategies is conventional but increasingly arbitrary. The most sophisticated hardware is worthless unless programs enable it to perform its intended functions. Logically, then, computer systems should be thought of as composed of hardware and software components, which are then considered together as a whole. Firms prepared to program all their systems from scratch can ignore the software aspect to a large extent and concentrate on hardware selection. For the vast majority of organizations, however, this approach is completely unrealistic. As software becomes increasingly sophisticated and as the cost of software becomes an ever larger part of the cost of the total system, it becomes less and less feasible to consider hardware and software as separate issues. This distinction only facilitates our exposition; we will endeavor, however, to make the connections as clear as possible.

A major decision in system selection and development is the use of off-the-shelf program packages versus individually written programs tailored to the users' needs. Such packages may be classified into three types: system controls, problem solvers, and applications. *System control packages*, or operating systems, are usually supplied by the equipment manufacturer. They are almost invariably adopted with the equipment because the cost of developing such packages is far beyond the reach of any but the largest organizations. In some specific and unusual situations the need to modify operating systems substantially may arise. However, such modification invariably reduces the manufacturer's guarantee and levels of support and service.

Problem-solving packages include simulation models, forecasting models, and computerized decision models such as linear programming, mathematical programming in general, and statistical analysis packages. Many of the most popular packages in this field were developed by users, especially universities, made available to other users, and eventually achieved widespread use.

Least progress has been made with *application packages* because of the difficulties in building packages of sufficient generality to satisfy the varying needs of a number of organizations, each with a unique personality; lack of portability of programs developed for one environment into another; and problems in integrating packages, which are generally built to stand alone, with other applications. In some areas, however, applications are highly structured, either by their nature or by the requirements of outside agencies and lend themselves more readily to incorporation in generalized packages; in such areas the use of standard packages has become quite widespread. Examples include bill-of-material processing, production scheduling, payroll preparation, and billing and accounts receivable.

Obviously, software acquisition should be considered in conjunction with hardware acquisition and the organization should look for the hardware-software package best suited to its needs, based on which programs the organization is prepared to write itself and which it can purchase as packages. Thus there may be trade-offs between hardware and software specifications of the systems considered. A technologically more advanced system may be passed by in favor of a less advanced system that provides more of the software the organization needs; other organizations may decide that hardware sophistication is their greatest need and will be prepared to write large quantities of software. For large organizations or for organizations with widely used applications, some costs may be passed on by developing packages jointly with an equipment manufacturer who will then market it, such as the joint development by American Airlines and IBM of the SABRE airline reservation system.[11] As usual, each organization in each situation is faced with the problem of choosing the best solution for its own contingencies.[12]

Organizational Requirements

An MIS is a complex assemblage of hardware and software put together by groups of people involved in the development project. Personnel deployment raises several questions about the relationships among them and between them and the organization, such as the location and structuring of the information-processing function in the organization, the study group, the steering group, the corporate computer staff, the organization of the system development function, the interface between the MIS project and users, and the use of external assistance and services.

The worst course an organization can take is to refrain from making explicit organizational decisions, leaving problems to be solved on an ad hoc basis, according to temporary needs and power structures. Experience has shown that organizational problems should be solved consciously and formally. The most common solutions to organizational problems and the circumstances in which they are effective are discussed below.

Location in the Organization

Historically, data-processing units have undergone a process of rapid appreciation. From automating small, well-defined clerical tasks, they have been upgraded to the design and implementation of top-management control and planning systems. Gibson and Nolan view this development as a step-wise process composed of four stages, paralleling the stages of information system development—initiation, expansion, formalization, and maturity.[13] In the initiation stage, the EDP unit is located in the department whose applications are the first to be computerized, usually accounting. In the last stage, maturity of information systems, the information unit is a separate, autonomous functional area.

In the early sixties, most organizations placed the responsibility for computers in the accounting department. At that time computers were regarded as machines for automating clerical work, not as decision tools. The nature of the work at that time (analyzing transaction systems and writing computer programs) was perceived to be related to the skills existing in the accounting department, as were the processes that were automated. This practice is strongly opposed by Hanold, who distinguishes clearly between accounting and finance and firmly advocates locating the information function in finance.[14] Hanold views accounting as an evaluative system, whose main task is to evaluate management's performance post factum, rather than a management function. Because the "accounting fraternity" is bound by standard accounting procedures and has obligations to the board of directors, shareholders, and the public, accounting departments analyze and present rather than manage. Hanold recommends that the MIS department be located in the domain of responsibility of the chief finance officer because finance is related to top management and deals with uncertainty both inside and outside the organization.

Formerly, the general practice was to establish information units where the initial applications were. This practice, convenient at the beginning, creates serious problems later. First, the location within a specific function inhibits and delays application outside this jurisdiction. Integration of applications across functional areas is also inhibited so that the process of transforming the data-processing group into an MIS function is also hindered. When the scope of applications does broaden to cover additional functional areas, top management usually extracts the MIS unit from the functional area in which it is embedded to create an autonomous group. This structural change at the top of the organization reduces the power of one executive while creating a new locus of power. Many organizations have paid the price of this change in terms of hostility, lack of cooperation, and management turnover.

This evolutionary process, dependent on time and maturity, was almost universal in the past and is still very common. However, organizations newly embarking on the road to MIS are not necessarily restricted to the historic pattern of development and should tailor the process to their development strategy. Organizations consciously adopting a bottom-up strategy coupled with data-base development might choose to repeat the conventional pattern. But even then an autonomous unit would better facilitate integration and the initiation of projects for higher levels of management. An organization whose MIS target focuses on a top-down development strategy, coupled with a purpose oriented on planning and control models, should also, in our opinion, establish an autonomous unit, but might prefer to locate it in corporate planning according to its specific needs and problems.

It should be clear by now that we strongly favor an autonomous status for the information function in the organization. This point of view is not particularly heretical because, in practice, MIS are becoming recognized as an independent area of management. The status we advocate for the MIS unit also leads to the conclusion that the responsibility for MIS must be very high in the organizational hierarchy. As we point out in chapter 5, the manager of MIS should rank at most three levels below the chief executive of the organization. Only this combination of independence and status will permit the MIS unit to perform its function of integrating the data and decision processes of the organization.

Organization of the Information Systems
Development Function

The organization of the information systems development function is yet another manifestation of the centralization versus decentralization issue, this time in the context of the systems development resource. The decision concerning the organization of the people developing information systems is naturally inseparable from the decision on hardware centralization or decentralization, an issue dealt with in the section on equipment strategies. This connection, however, does not mean that the solution must be identical for both material and human resources. If we think of centralization and decentralization as two distinct conditions, rather than as a continuum, five organizational combinations of hardware and system development resources can be identified:

1. Centralized hardware with decentralized system development and programming
2. Centralized hardware and programming with decentralized systems development
3. Decentralized hardware with centralized development and programming
4. Centralized hardware, systems, and programming with directly linked satellite installations
5. Centralized hardware, systems and programming with autonomous satellite installations[15]

This list shows, first, that almost any combination of equipment and development resource organizations is possible, and second, the development resource itself may be divided into two separate groups—analysis and programming—with any possible combination of organizations between them. Again, each organization must choose the combination of these functions that best suits its particular circumstances. Since there are so many possibilities, we shall point out some of the advantages and disadvantages of each form of organization rather than suggest specific solutions.

Advantages of Centralization.

Centralization permits uniform reporting systems and so facilitates company-wide consolidation of operating results.

Centralized management of the system function can improve coordination of the information system as a functional entity and facilitates the retention of well-qualified and well-motivated professionals because of the greater leeway in providing status, promotion, and state-of-the-art technology in larger groupings.

Centralization may provide greater flexibility for the total organization by separating the information system function from other functions, which may then be changed while information system development is largely shielded from the disruptions caused by such changes.

Disadvantages of Centralization.

The advantages of centralization are achieved at the cost of greater system complexity, higher communication outlays, and a possible loss of sight of users' needs through concentration on overall corporate objectives,

Too much centralization may lead to bureaucratization of the system development function and reduce its responsiveness, a problem compounded by isolating systems people from functional management.

Advantages of Decentralization.

Decentralization heightens familiarity and sensitivity of systems developers to local problems and promotes rapid response to local needs.

Decentralization can sometimes provide better opportunities for management development because more managers are exposed to the issues involved in information system development.

Decentralization mitigates the "scapegoat function"—the tendency to blame a remote and anthropomorphic computer for all problems and errors, whatever their real cause.

Decentralization provides greater autonomy and places profit and loss responsibility with the local manager, who is in the best position to evaluate benefits.

Disadvantages of Decentralization. The disadvantages of decentralization are the obverse of the advantages of centralization.

There are several ideological calls in the literature for more centralization of information systems development, while others claim that such centralization is impossible. The general approach to this issue, however, seems to be highly pragmatic. From the systems point of view, centralization is almost invariably called for, especially in geographically dispersed organizations, where it may be a major step towards presenting management with timely information from widely spread operating units. The more extreme centralization becomes, however, the more effective the disadvantages of centralization become. There is, therefore, an optimal degree of centralization in any organizational context. This approach is supported by the empirically observed fact that companies generally organize computer systems in conformance with their traditional plans of organization. Those which do not experience abnormal difficulties.[16]

The tendency to configure information systems in accordance with general corporate philosophy has led to the development of a "hybrid" organization with shared control. This form is currently the most popular; one survey showed that 20 percent of organizations now have highly decentralized control of information systems, in 32.5 percent it is highly centralized, while in 46.5 percent of organizations some form of hybrid organization is favored.[17] Thus the realities of life in organizations seem to demand some mix of centralization and decentralization that permits enjoyment of some of the advantages of both types of structure while avoiding the worst disadvantages of each.

The Study Group

The idea that the time has come to develop an MIS for some purpose somewhere in an organization may come from operational managers who think that it might enable them to do their job better; it might originate in top management, which needs better planning and control tools; or the initiative may be taken by the information systems group, which sees an opportunity to provide an additional service or to make additional use of existing data. Whatever the source of the proposal, the first step management should take is to establish a study group to determine its feasibility. The objective of such a study is, first of all, to determine whether the proposal is consistent with organizational policies and with the general situation of the organization. At Weyerhaeuser, for example, a study group determined that the development of MIS was mandatory if the company was to maintain its leadership in the industry.[18] This is a clear case of consistency with the organizational policy of leadership in the industry.

The next step for the study group is to make the evaluations recommended in chapters 2 and 3. It should examine the environment of the proposed system to determine whether it is benevolent or can be made sufficiently so. If the examination of the environment yields positive results, the proposal should then be examined in light of the organization's MIS target. If this is the first MIS to be considered by the organization, now is the time to formulate the target. If the target already exists and the proposed system is to be part of an ongoing program of development, the study group should then determine whether the system is consistent with the target in terms of the strategy and purpose that have been adopted and what priority it should have. Finally, the study group should determine the economic and technical feasibility of the proposal.

This initial study is geared to evaluating the benefits of the proposed system to the organization as a result of improving operations and increasing profits. Thus it is essential that operating management be well represented because they are better able to make these evaluations than are information experts (see our discussion in chapter 7). An early survey found that in companies with successful information systems, operating management played a strong role in project selection and planning, whereas in average companies, technical management tends to dominate.[19]

The Steering Committee

Whereas the study group is an ad hoc committee established for evaluating a specific proposal, the steering committee, which takes over where the study group leaves off, is a permanent group invested with the responsibility for continuing project supervision and guidance. In many cases, the study group is reappointed or reconstituted as a steering committee; often this recommendation originates in the study group itself. Especially in an ongoing MIS program the functions of the study group may be incorporated in the steering committee, which may set up subcommittee study groups as necessary.

Establishing a top-level, permanent steering committee is recommended as soon as the EDP function matures to the status of MIS development or when MIS implementation is being considered. It should include the following functions:

Examining information system policies, objectives, and priorities and making appropriate recommendations

Identifying potentially needed and profitable projects, or having proposals for such projects examined when they originate elsewhere

Projecting manpower, hardware and software requirements

Estimating and proposing budget allocations

Guiding and controlling project development, especially reviews to ensure that projects are on schedule and within budget

The steering committee should be composed of high-level executives, supported by experts; the higher the level of executives involved the better. The committee is a channel to the MIS unit, conveying the information needs of the organization. It is also a line of communication for the MIS director to the top of the organization, enabling him to explain the special needs of his unit and enabling him to gain support for innovative ideas and for resource allocation. All major functional areas must be represented on such a committee because sooner or later each functional area will be linked with MIS both as users and as sources of inputs. Early incorporation of an appreciation of functional processes and needs will pay dividends in later stages of development.

The role of the steering committee is well illustrated by McFarlan.[20] A division of a major aerospace company established a steering committee to review the priorities and progress of an MIS. Some time later the steering committee was abandoned as unworkable, but after "a sharp disruption in communications" it was reinstated. It was composed of eight vice-presidents, met once a month, and was engaged in establishing policy for the project. In a survey of fifteen companies, twelve exhibited the same basic features as described in this case. Thus the steering committee serves another important role as a "safety valve" for users' pressures. In addition to serving as a medium for attaining high-level user involvement in system development (discussed in chapter 7), the steering committee also plays its role in encouraging positive attitudes towards MIS by demonstrating top management support for the effort (discussed in chapter 5). Thus in addition to its overt role in project guidance, the steering committee has an important psychological role in modifying organizational attitudes and behaviors.

Corporate Computer Staff

The steering committee is a group of managers that provides the interface between organizational policies and information system content for the MIS group. The corporate computer staff provides an interface for technical policies and coordination. The need for a corporate computer staff and its functions depends on the degree of centralization or decentralization of information system development. The more centralized information system development is, the smaller the need for a corporate information function at the staff level; in the extreme case of complete centralization of MIS development, the director of information systems usually also performs the staff function of providing technical advice to top management in this field.

When the organization is decentralized, as are its information systems and implementation units, central guidance becomes important. A lack of central technical guidance leads to a slippage in the status of information systems in the organization, generates uncoordinated efforts and overcapacity in computing equipment, leads to lack of standardization, and prevents attainment of the advantages of presenting a united front to hardware and software vendors.

Decentralized organizations with highly qualified corporate computer staffs are more likely to succeed in MIS development than those without them. The corporate staff should have superior technical skills and be effective in working with nontechnical personnel, mainly managers. The functions of the computer staff are to advise management and steering committees on technical issues such as computer and software acquisition; to institute and control operating and documentation standards; to control the efficiency of computer operations; to suggest ways of rationalizing decentralized computer operations by sharing facilities, standardizing equipment and transferring personnel for optimal deployment; to negotiate centrally with vendors to achieve maximum leverage; to monitor the progress of projects; and to point out opportunities that may arise from new technologies, new applications, or new situations inside or outside the organization.

Organization of The System Development Function

There are two major forms of organization for the implementors of MIS development projects. The more conventional form is by functions; analysis, programming, and operations groups assign personnel to specific tasks as the need arises and are responsible for them both organizationally and for their technical performance. A programmer may be simultaneously engaged in writing two or three programs, each for a different system. The advantage of this arrangement is that it promises maximal utilization of personnel, since, when there is a slack period for the people working on one project, they can be assigned work from another.

The alternative form of organization is by project teams; personnel are assigned to a project for its duration, with no other responsibilities during that period. The advantage of this method is that project leaders are better able to manage their projects when they have full control of the people working on them. Furthermore, membership in a project team fosters identification with the project and motivates greater efforts for its success. When the project is complete, which may include running-in the working system, the team is disbanded and its members assigned to new projects.

No clear evidence indicates that either organization achieves better results than the other. On the contrary, there are reports of successful development under both forms. The rule that any form of organizational change accompanied by an interest in the personnel involved increases performance also seems to apply in this case, as evidenced by several reports of sudden changes from one form to the other.

As in many previous cases, we suspect that the prime determinant of success is the degree of consistency of the organizational form chosen with the nature and structure of the firm as a whole. A well-structured and mature organization aiming at highly integrated MIS, where organizational behavior and the environment are quite stable, will benefit more from a structured and functional MIS organization. This type of organization will not function well in a dynamic and fragmented milieu. Where there are many large projects with little interaction between them, the organization is growing and changing rapidly, and planning is difficult and uncertain, project team organization is preferable.

The User Interface

No matter how decentralized a system's equipment and development staff organization, there will always be users in remote locations (geographically or organizationally) who are not in contact with it. In these cases it is necessary to provide the local management with suport in the identification and solution of problems. This support is especially important during the project development process to ensure that the remote units have a clear voice in the planning unit and that their particular needs receive attention during the system's formative stages—not when it is already operational and it is, perhaps, too late.

Though most essential during system development, remotely located system staff can also play an important role after systems become operational. Then their role is to assist in the local maintenance of systems as an integral part of the users' areas. Remote staff are then in daily contact with local problems, they can find solutions to them, and they can initiate and design special purpose systems or modules specific to the periphery and negotiate their implementation with the main system. Thus the remote system personnel are both local troubleshooters and communications links with the central computer and development resource.

It has been recommended that remote locations be manned by at least a department manager and one system-trained person, with as many technical support personnel as dictated by the workload at the site.[21] Interestingly, the more centralized the system resources, the more remote users and the greater the needs for this decentralized attachment of systems people to field locations. Thus, high centralization of computers and development leads to widespread decentralization of resources for liaison; this factor also indicates that there is an optimal degree of centralization which brings system resources sufficiently close to users so that a massive liaison effort is not required.

External Assistance

A major alternative in the field of organizational arrangements for project development is the employment of external assistance. Qualified systems and software people claim high salaries and generally prefer working in large information system units; thus organizations with limited MIS plans find themselves faced by demand for high salaries for average talent, which they may have difficulty releasing when the project is complete. Furthermore, in some stable industries, top management salaries are traditionally low and hiring a highly paid MIS director may destroy a carefully balanced structure of management remuneration. Firms facing such problems should consider hiring external assistance in project development to reduce commitments and destabilization to a minimum.

Several types of organizations offer information system development services, including:

MIS consultants, who specialize in system conceptualization, planning, advice on computer and software acquisition, and guiding and controlling system design and implementation. Typically MIS consultants serve on study groups and steering committees as technical advisers or as personal advisors to executives, but rarely engage in actual implementation.

Management consultants, who also provide EDP services. They provide many of the same services as MIS consultants, but usually with a more functional and less technical orientation. Many consulting firms offer both general management and specialized MIS consulting.

Accounting firms specializing in auditing, coupled with EDP services, concentrate mainly in administrative systems tied to the accounting function in the organization. They are rarely constituted to provide services connected with management information systems in the sense we have defined.

Service bureaus that specialize in hardware services but also supply software are primarily an alternative to in-house hardware systems, but may offer standardized software packages for common applications. If their hardware is to be employed, they will usually also program the system and may even do the systems analysis.

Software houses, whose main business is vending sophisticated general purpose software systems and developing specialized software systems to order, often provide "turnkey" services in which the customer receives a working system.

Computer manufacturers usually provide some form of consulting service in system selection and development and may even undertake to program systems in certain circumstances.

Each type of consultant specializes in a somewhat different area. Thus firms should first determine exactly what kind of assistance they need and which kind of consulting services firm is best qualified to provide it.

In the mid-sixties, a survey found that the use of computer manufacturers as consultants exceeded the combined use of all other kinds of consultants.[22] This pattern has apparently not changed. Management views the work of the representatives of the computer manufacturers as "free advice," ignoring or discounting their legitimate biases. Furthermore, when several manufacturers are consulted in an adversary situation, much valuable information may come to light.

An important advantage of external consultants is their freedom of access to top management. As discussed in chapter 5, top management support of the MIS effort is an important ingredient of success. Though internal staff may often have difficulty in scheduling frequent meetings with top management, external consultants usually have easy access—which contributes to their effectiveness. MIS chiefs frequently have their organizations hire consultants to achieve this kind of access. Consultants also foster an aura of objectivity, which may help the MIS chief working with them to get his ideas accepted.

The nature of the industry, its precedents, and the application all contribute to the decision to employ external assistance. However, the size of the organization is the single most important factor in this decision. Larger organizations have less to gain from outside help. The size of internal operations with their attendant flexibility in deployment, the expertise that accumulates in large organizations, and the individuality of organizations all leave little incentive to employ consultants, except perhaps in some window-dressing roles. Because smaller organizations are less flexible and less able to undertake complex projects, they find the use of consultants more attractive.

External help should never be considered a complete substitute for internal staff. Even when virtually all of a project is contracted out, the specifications and control of the project should be firmly in the hands of an executive from the user organization. When organizations base themselves totally on outsiders, the information needs of managers are usually not understood, the special nature of the organization is not captured in the systems, and outputs do not fit needs or encourage use. Though external assistance may often be useful or even mandatory, it must be managed and coordinated by an internal MIS unit, no matter how rudimentary. The greater the extent to which the organization is involved in project development, the more likely it is to succeed.

The main points in this chapter and their implications for MIS management are summarized in table 4-1.

Table 4-1
Summary of MIS Project Variables

Variables	Conclusions
Stages of the MIS project	The MIS project is a process composed of eight execution phases, each accompanied or terminated by a management control phase. The more complete the sequence of execution-control cycles, the greater the likelihood of MIS project success. The input to the project process is the MIS target, which is first translated into specifications, followed by planning and scheduling, staffing, analysts' study and design, programming, implementation and installation, operation, and support and maintenance.
	Critical control phases relate to specification, design, and programming.
	Each stage should be thoroughly documented.
Equipment strategy	Equipment strategy is concerned with the definition of computer capabilities, method of selection, form of acquisition, and equipment deployment.
	Because computer capabilities are fixed in the short run, attention should be given to the need for growth in capacity. The time devoted to computer selection should be restricted. Too much attention to the selection process diverts attention from other important topics.
	Equipment may be installed in-house (purchased or rented) or services purchased from service bureaus. In-house equipment provides autonomous control; service bureaus are recommended for small organizations or transition periods.
	Hardware deployment possibilities are a central complex, regional facilities, and networks, especially minicomputer networks. The deployment should be consistent with organizational structure, philosophy, and needs.

Table 4-1 (cont.)

Software strategy	Hardware and software are becoming increasingly inseparable. A major decision is between the use of off-the-shelf packages versus programming. System control packages are almost invariably bought, problem-solving packages are frequently acquired, while application packages are usually self-produced or made to order.
Organizational arrangements	Suitable organizational arrangements for the various groups involved in the project development are important to project success.
	The MIS function should be autonomous and report to a high-level executive.
	The degree of centralization of the implementation group should conform to the traditional plan of the organization. A study group, composed of managers and experts, should determine the feasibility of project proposals (environment analysis and MIS target definition).
	A permanent steering committee guides and supervises the project. The higher the level of the members of the committee, the greater its effectiveness. A corporate computer staff of technical experts is required in organizations choosing to decentralize implementation.
	Growing and dynamic organizations are advised to adopt a project team organization for implementors. Stable and formalized organizations will do better with functional organization of implementors.
	In centralized systems, development personnel should be integrated in remote locations to provide an interface with users. External assistance can be obtained from MIS consultants, management consultants, accounting firms, service bureaus, software houses, and computer manufacturers. Smaller organizations may benefit from external assistance. Consultants have direct access to top management, thus increasing their effectivity.

Notes

1. E.E. David, in Naur, Peter, and Brian Randell (eds.), *Software Engineering*, Report on a Conference sponsored by the NATO Science Committee, NATO, Scientific Affairs Division, January 1969, p. 67.

2. Ibid, p. 83.

3. For a good technical discussion of advanced programming techniques see Brian W. Kernighan and P.J. Plauger, *Software Tools* (Reading, Mass.: Addison-Wesley, 1976).

4. For a discussion of techniques for system evaluation see Eric D. Carlson, "Evaluating the Impact of Information Systems," *Management Informatics*, vol. 3, no. 2 (April 1974), pp. 57-67.

5. For full discussions of information system documentation see Keith R. London, *Documentation Standards* (New York: Petrocelli Books, (1974), or J. Van Duyn, *Documentation Manual* (Philadelphia: Auerbach, 1972). A concise suggestion for programming standards is Franz Selig, "Documentation Standards," in *Software Engineering*, pp. 209-211.

6. For further discussion of this approach see Phillip Ein-Dor, "A Dynamic Approach to Computer System Selection," *Datamation*, vol. 23, no. 6 (June 1977), pp. 103-108.

7. John T. Garrity, "Top Management and Computer Profits," *Harvard Business Review*, vol. 41, no. 4 (July-August 1963), pp. 6-12, 172-174.

8. For a discussion of selection procedures of this type see Gordon Davis, *Introduction to Electronic Computers*, 2nd ed. (New York: McGraw-Hill, 1971), pp. 607-625.

9. Mayford L. Roark, "Centralization Versus Decentralization of the MIS Effort." *Proceedings: The Second Annual Conference of The Society for Management Information Systems* (Washington, D.C., September 1970).

10. W. David Gardner, "Major Bank Replaces Large Mainframe With Minicomputers," *Datamation*, vol. 22, no. 8 (August 1976), pp. 106 ff.

11. William E. Jenkins, "Airline Reservation Systems," *Datamation*, vol. 15, no. 3 (March 1969), pp. 29-32.

12. For a full discussion of software strategies see Suzan Wooldridge, *Software Selection* (Philadelphia: Auerbach, 1973).

13. Cyrus F. Gibson and Richard L. Nolan, "Managing the Four Stages of EDP Growth," *Harvard Business Review*, vol. 52, no. 1 (January-February 1974), pp. 76-88.

14. Terrance Hanold, "An Executive View of MIS," *Datamation*, vol. 18, no. 11 (November 1972), pp. 65-71.

15. J. Milutinovich and H.A. Kanter, "Organizing the MIS Department," *Journal of Systems Management*, vol. 26, no. 4 (April 1975), pp. 36-41.

16. Garrity "Top Management and Computer Profits."

17. C.H. Kriebel, "Discussion Comments on Emery," *Data Base*, vol. 5, nos. 2, 3, and 4 (Winter 1973), pp. 11-13.

18. R.A. Kronenberg, "Weyerhaeuser's Management Information System," *Datamation*, vol. 13, no. 5 (May 1967), pp. 28-30.

19. Garrity, "Top Management and Computer Profits."

20. F. Warren McFarlan, "Problems in Planning the Information System," *Harvard Business Review*, vol. 49, no. 2 (March-April 1971), pp. 74-89.

21. Milutinovich and Kanter, "Organizing the MIS Department."
22. Garrity, "Top Management and Computer Profits."

Suggested Readings

Gibson, Cyrus F., and Nolan, Richard L. "Managing the Four Stages of EDP Growth." *Harvard Business Review,* vol. 52, no. 1 (January-February 1974), pp. 76-88.

Jenkins, William E. "Airline Reservation Systems." *Datamation,* vol. 15, no. 3 (March 1969), pp. 29-32.

Kronenberg, R.A. "Weyerhaeuser's Management Information System." *Datamation,* vol. 13, no. 5 (May 1967), pp. 28-30.

Roark, Mayford L. 'Centralization Versus Decentralization of the MIS Effort." *Proceedings: The Second Annual Conference of The Society for Management Information Systems* (Washington, D.C., September 1970).

5 Executive Responsibility

Many people in the organization play important roles in the development, implementation, operation, and evolution of management information systems. These may be divided into three main groups—executives bearing responsibility for the systems, implementors of the systems, and users. Chapters 5, 6, and 7 are each devoted to one of the three groups. An additional chapter on the human aspects of MIS (chapter 8) discusses the interrelationships between these groups.

Executives who assume or are assigned responsibility for information systems have a critical impact on the course of MIS in their organizations. This chapter deals with the roles of executives not formally part of the information system function and their responsibilities towards the MIS. It is useful to distinguish clearly between two types of relationships linking executives and management information systems: the responsibility relationship and the user relationship. The former deals with managers' supervision of the MIS as a unit of the organization and the latter with the interactions of managers with the system as users. These relationships are not necessarily equivalent. An executive may use a system he does not supervise, he may supervise a system he does not use personally, or he may both supervise and use a system. The responsibility relationship is the topic of this chapter. The executive as user is discussed in chapter 7.

The Aspects of Executive Responsibility

The impact of responsible executives on MIS is felt in three areas—rank, association, and relationships (figure 5-1). *Rank* refers to the level of executive responsible for MIS; how "top" is the top management association with the system? The executive's *association* with the MIS is expressed in the time devoted to it and the skill level acquired, which in turn determine the MIS functions that management is able to perform. The level of association also works indirectly through the perceptions it generates in other members of the organization. Finally, the *relationships* of top management with other groups in the organization directly connected with MIS, such as implementors and users, have an effect on their success and failure. Because these relationships are reciprocal, discussion of them is deferred until all three groups concerned have been identified and discussed.

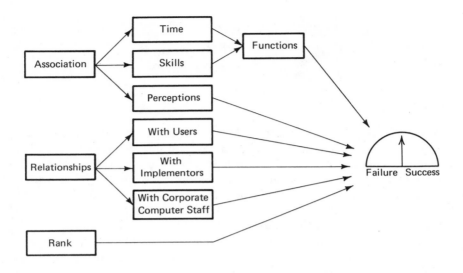

Figure 5-1. Executive Contributions to Success and Failure of Management Information Systems

Location and Rank of the Responsible Executive

In the following sections of this chapter we refer to top management as a whole, and indeed all senior managers have a role to play in furthering the development of information systems. In practice, however, only one manager is personally responsible for any particular information system. Historically, electronic data processing usually began and evolved in the accounting function of the organization; as a result, the controller was usually assigned responsibility for the system. As other functions in the organization developed computerized information systems, either additional executives were assigned responsibility for their own systems, or else information systems began reporting to a higher level, superior to the functional levels. With the tendency for MIS to serve higher levels of management and with increasing integration of systems across functional boundaries, the tendency to upgrade the organizational level to which the information system function reports has become widespread. This upgrading is necessary to permit information systems to operate across traditional functions. Thus the location of the responsible executive and his rank tend to be mutually dependent; location within a function implies a lower rank whereas an extrafunctional location implies a higher rank. The question, then, is how top should the top management formally responsible for MIS be?

In chapter 1, we indicated that many management information systems, serving various levels and areas of management, may co-exist in any organization. There are MIS for functional areas, planning, and control at plant, division, group, and corporate levels. This fact is often obscured by references to "the MIS," accompanied by recommendations that the MIS function should report to the chief executive officer of the corporation. This may be true for a *top management* information system, but because there are managers and a level of management relevant to each management information system, it is clear that the MIS should be supervised at the level of management and in the area which it serves. Both experience and several surveys suggest that the likelihood of MIS success declines rapidly the lower the rank of the responsible executive; it is virtually negligible if the MIS chief is more than two levels below the chief officer of the organization. Though many writers are suggestive rather than specific on this issue, those who are explicit discuss the corporate level and suggest only a narrow range of possible solutions. In the corporation, either the chief executive officer, a vice-president, or a director of management information services should be responsible for MIS.

It is helpful to consider the problem of executive responsibility within Nolan's framework of the stages of the system development—initiation, expansion, formalization, and maturity.[1] Top management involvement is needed in all these stages, but the third stage, formalization, requires that the MIS department be autonomous and report to a vice-president or even to the president himself. In this stage, the financial commitment, as well as the diversity of applications, call for direction from the highest levels. Circumstances seem to dictate this solution and several field studies have found that the rank of executive responsible for information systems rises as the system matures.

In many corporations, decisions on computers and information systems are kept at the highest level. Terrance Hanold described his policy as president of Pillsbury:

Pillsbury's corporate policy obliges each of its operating firms "to obtain full utilization and value from Pillsbury's Business Information System." To ensure this result the policy provides that "the General Manager must assume responsibility for the definition of the information and processing requirements of his operation. . . ." This same concept is carried to the corporate level. Our policy states that "Certain affairs of the Pillsbury Company are inseparable from its Executive Office." Among them is the Pillsbury Business Information System. Without immediate control of the design and operation of this system in its entirety, the Executive Office cannot effectively function. It is for this reason the PBIS reports directly to the Executive office. . . . Each functional information system is the responsibility of the functional management in matters of design, structure and purpose. The MIS is the responsibility of the general and executive management.[2]

Surveys indicate such policies are by no means uncommon.

However, experts in every area of management from corporate planning through business-community relations to labor relations advocate the involvement and supervision, in their area, of the chief executive officer. It is, of course, impossible for a single person to personally supervise so many functions. Like other top management systems, MIS, in some phases of development (initiation, critical change, new approach) may need the personal intervention of the chief executive, while in other phases (stabilization, routine) they may operate successfully under a vice-president. The solution is that the chief executive officer will assume personal responsibility for MIS (and other top management systems) in transition periods, while delegating responsibility to a vice-president when circumstances permit. Because MIS are relatively new and changing rapidly, it is not surprising to find considerable involvement of chief executives.

In many corporations, the information system function reports to a senior vice-president. For example, in Merck and Company following considerable expansion of the information system function, the responsibility for MIS was detached from the controller's office and a vice-president for management information systems appointed. A similar process occurred in the Arkwright-Boston Manufacturers Mutual Insurance Company, where a vice-president for MIS reports to a senior administrative vice-president.

Dearden recommends an organizational deployment in which the controller, the treasurer, the computer and systems group, and a number of other officers report to a senior administrative vice-president.[3] Its advantages for information system management are that an administrative vice-president can be more objective than the controller, who is involved in his own specific applications. Thus this arrangement provides an alternative to supervision by the controller, while still maintaining close relations with the controller's office. Furthermore, it facilitates establishing task groups to handle nonrecurrent, urgent, and otherwise difficult systems. Nevertheless, Dearden circumscribes the authority of the central office to deal with functional information systems. In his opinion, marketing, manufacturing, and the other functional areas should all be responsible for their own information systems. The administrative vice-president would not be responsible for the total management information system but would coordinate when interface problems arise. In this conception, the administrative vice-president controls and coordinates, but does not initiate.

No matter what particular organizational arrangement is adopted, the evidence is overwhelming that the probability of MIS success is smaller the lower the rank of the responsible executive. Because the manager of information systems does not appoint the executive to whom he reports, he may face a real problem. It is the duty of the MIS manager to arouse the interest of the highest echelons in the organization and to establish direct lines of communication to them. In a recent case of information system failure that we studied, the leaders of the information system group noted that one reason for the failure was their inability to induce the involvement of the top management of the organization. Establishing such involvement is one of the key roles of the information system manager.

Association

Top management association contributes, or is essential, to the success of management information systems, as shown in surveys of hundreds of information systems in fields as diverse as business, hospitals, and police departments; the same conclusion is drawn in numerous case studies of single organizations. Conversely, a number of authorities have diagnosed a lack of top management association as contributing to poor MIS performance.

The types of relationship considered beneficial have been expressed in many different words, including "participation," "involvement," "commitment," "support," "vested interest," "concern," "understanding," "appreciation," "champion," "belief," and "enthusiasm." All these words individually and collectively convey a sense of sympathetic patronage or benign guidance.

Efforts should be made to create an atmosphere conducive to top management's involvement with the MIS. MIS development should be structured so that top management involvement is built-in to some extent. One method is to employ outside consultants, because in addition to their expertise, they frequently have much easier access to top level executives than do employees of the organization and involve them in planning and use of the system.

The milestone approach to system development is another method of achieving involvement. A milestone is a date, or point in the process, at which a specific decision is required of management. No further progress is possible without management review of the project at that juncture and the adoption of an overt decision in regard to the next phase, which includes scheduling the next milestone. Such milestones force management's involvement, even when it would rather play a passive role with respect to information systems.

Another tactic that has been found effective in generating management interest is a development plan based on incremental progress rather than on a total effort. The emphasis is on meeting current needs by modifying existing systems rather than on a large-scale effort to build a total system. Because the incremental approach promises management quick returns for a relatively small effort in a system that they already know and understand, the motivation to become involved is quite high. Large, all-inclusive corporate models, however, are difficult for management to understand, and the payoffs are usually far off in the future; in such circumstances, it is difficult to motivate management to become closely involved.

Necessity and Sufficiency

Evidence on the importance of top management association is abundant and persuasive and should guide MIS management. Nevertheless, the involvement of top management is neither absolutely necessary for success nor, of course, is it sufficient to guarantee success.

Not every top management is ready to support MIS efforts, and some may even oppose them. Does such alienation doom MIS to failure? Despite its desirability, top management support is not absolutely indispensable. One survey of twenty management information systems in three large organizations (a government engineering unit, an aerospace corporation, and the headquarters of a large conglomerate) found that 16 percent of the thirty-three people interviewed stated that upper management was neither supportive nor negative; a further 16 percent stated that their systems had been opposed by management but were implemented despite the opposition. Three conditions are needed to permit the construction of systems against the objections of top management: the system should be confined to a particular function rather than being comprehensive; the MIS staff needs a great deal of autonomy; and resources must be available for independent action.

Just as the positive involvement of top management is not absolutely essential for successful MIS, such involvement alone is not enough to guarantee success. In many cases systems have had the blessing of top management but implementation was nevertheless retarded. Much of this book is devoted to identifying factors that, if unfavorable, can lead to failure. One of our basic conclusions is that no single critical variable determines the success or failure of management information systems. The outcome is always the result of complex interplay between many variables determining the starting point, the development process, and the final state of the system.

Reasons for Lack of Involvement

The main reasons for the underinvolvement of top management in MIS development and operation are a lack of appreciation of computerized systems, feelings of being threatened by them, and the amount of time they demand.

Both scholars and practitioners have suggested that management's lack of involvement results from a lack of appreciation of systems, although neither involvement nor appreciation were operationally defined and the suggestion was not supported by formal evidence. Swanson, however, has defined appreciation: "The MIS appreciation of a manager consists of his manifold of beliefs about the relative value of the MIS as a means of inquiry."[4] A survey disclosed that appreciation of MIS and involvement with MIS are co-produced, so that managers who are involved will be appreciative and those who are uninvolved will also be unappreciative. Because appreciation and involvement are co-produced, it follows that managers who are appreciative become involved and increase their appreciation, while those who are unappreciative remain uninvolved and retain their lack of appreciation. Understanding is thought to be the connecting link between appreciation and involvement. Managers who understand computers are appreciative and become involved. Involvement increases understanding and so strengthens appreciation.

Lack of involvement is also fostered when managers perceive that the information system threatens their decision-making functions and prerogatives of exercising managerial judgment. Middle management's fear of being replaced by computers has been frequently reported, as has their perception that personal contact with the computer (by means of displays, for example) will be interpreted as a loss of intuitive decision skills. Although top management obviously has less ground for this kind of fear, it is more than likely that, subconsciously at least, these factors deter greater involvement. An unwillingness to display ignorance has also been cited as keeping top managers from full involvement with information systems.

Management association with the MIS effort makes itself felt through the functions that management performs and through the perceptions that the degree of association engenders in other levels of the organization, especially in middle management.

The functions that management can and does perform can be measured by the time and the level of skills achieved. These two criteria structure our discussion of executive functions relating to MIS; next we will examine the effect of involvement on organizational perceptions.

Management Functions and Management Time

The functions that the executive responsible for MIS is required to perform are numerous and taxing. In the implementation of a management information system for research and development management in the Department of Defense it was reported that, during one phase, the senior executive responsible devoted up to 25 percent of his time to the project. This cost raises the threshold of motivation necessary for effective involvement and probably contributes to lack of involvement.

Top management time is one of the scarcest of organizational resources; why are such massive amounts of time required by information systems? The answer seems to lie in the extensive list of functions that top management is required to perform in exercising its responsibility to MIS. A synthesis of the various opinions of theorists and practitioners yields the following list of possible functions:

Defining information and processing requirements

Setting goals and appraising objectives, criteria, and priorities

Allocating resources and deciding on organizational arrangements to carry out the policy

Assigning responsibility to line and functional executives and verifying exercise of this responsibility

Evaluating project proposals

Initiating the design process, involvement in it, and control of it

Planning: reviewing plans and programs for the computer effort, guiding and supporting research and planning, and insisting that detailed plans are made an integral part of operating plans and budgets

Communicating desires on documentation

Controlling operations, reviewing and following through to see that planned results are achieved

This list of management functions operationalizes the concept of management involvement. The management that performs these functions, or at least some of them, is in fact involved.

As we pointed out earlier, a large portion of management time is needed to fill all these functions, time that is not always available. The relative importance of these functions must be decided—which are critical and which may be delegated to subordinates without imperiling the success of the systems. There is no consensus on this issue. Some of the areas considered most critical are setting goals, establishing priorities, defining requirements, and allocating resources. We will examine the arguments for each in turn.

Several surveys of firms with computerized information systems found that management has often abdicated its responsibility for goal definition. In these instances, goal definition devolves by default to information system experts. Because such experts are not strategically placed in the organization and are not aware of the real needs of management, they often develop systems for which there is no real use and such systems subsequently fail. Because technicians are unable to set goals consistent with organizational needs, management must "dirty its hands" and involve itself in goal determination to realize the full potential of information systems.

There are numerous opportunities for applying MIS in any organization. If management does not set priorities for selecting applications, this responsibility is also defaulted to the system technicians who lack the criteria for making such decisions. One study of ten computer-using companies showed that management was not involved in determining priorities in eight; as a result, information systems did not support the critical areas of business management.[5] In the other two cases, management insisted on a particular set of priorities, which would not otherwise have been chosen because other alternatives were more popular. As a result of management's stubbornness, an advanced stage of information system development was achieved in support of the critical areas of business operations.

In companies with top-down development of MIS, it is essential that top management outline the framework of the process. This framework should include a strategy for MIS development, the organizational deployment, and control processes. Such a framework implies that top management must itself initiate the design process—that is, it must delineate the organizational strategy, structure, and decision-making processes and ensure that the experts integrate these features into the system design.

A somewhat different approach states that top management has to ensure that all the functions we listed above are executed, but does not necessarily have to execute them personally. All the functions can be executed jointly with staff and line managers, except for resource allocation which is the prerogative of top management and the one function in which *only* top management takes part. Other functions may be delegated to lower echelons, under the supervision of top management.

In summary, it is clear that the executive responsible for MIS cannot possibly perform all these functions personally all the time. Therefore the responsible executive must tailor his involvement to fit the particular problems of the system in each period. Here, too, the stage theory of information system development is useful; the particular kind of involvement required of top management varies from one stage of development to the next. The task of the director of information systems is to channel executive action into those functions where it is most critical in each stage.

Management Functions and the Skills Factor

To perform the functions outlined in the previous section, the executive responsible must be endowed with considerable abilities, including the ability to correctly assess the potential of systems and to evaluate them, the ability to specify information requirements and decision rules, the ability to control systems, the ability to prepare plans and to stick to budgets, and the ability to seek out and identify significant projects.

The top manager needs two basic sets of skills. First, strong administrative skills are required for planning, problem identification, and budget control. Second, he must have a feel for systems and a knowledge of computer jargon, at least to the extent necessary for communication with computer personnel and for project evaluation.

In practice, management seems to have considerable difficulty in performing some managerial functions. One study found that in companies with successful information systems, top management had a balanced view of the potential of computers and the demands made on them.[6] In average companies, either the potential of computers was underrated or their technical requirements overrated. This difficulty in making correct assessments highlights the ignorance of the technology frequently exhibited by management and its consequent inability to evaluate information systems.

Some writers even suggest that management not only lacks technological competence, but also skill in dealing with information in general. Doubts have been raised whether managers know what information they need or how to use it when they have it. In a case quoted in *Fortune*, "few top managers could tell what kind of information they wanted or what they would do with it if they had it."[7]

In a recent experiment, 60 managers were set the task of designing an optimal information system for a theoretical firm with three geographically dispersed locations.[8] The problem was to determine which locations should monitor the environment and to which of the other locations they should report. In this case, 22 of the managers devised infeasible systems, 32 devised systems that could work but were suboptimal, while only 6 designed optimal systems. This work suggests that cognitive limitations may be a major factor leading to the inability to evaluate information systems.

An additional managerial deficiency is manifested in MIS control which seems to be less a problem of the ability of management to control than it is a problem of lack of standards. There is no generally accepted set of standards against which corporate management and MIS executives can evaluate their control procedures. Given this lack of an objective yardstick, there is a tendency to accept whatever is being done as correct.

The requisite skills portray a manager who is a generalist rather than a particularist and who understands the need to bring diverse elements of the organization together as a system. These skills and the capabilities inherent in them are required of top managers if, in addition to assuming responsibility for the MIS and devoting sufficient time, they are also to be qualified to exercise the responsibility effectively.

Management Association and Organizational Perceptions

It is not sufficient that there be a high level of management association with the MIS; it must also be perceived as such in the organization. The importance of having management support known in the organization was first identified by Garrity, who found that the attitude of top management was a good predictor of MIS success.[9] In those corporations where management's attitude was known to favor MIS, operating executives responded accordingly and became prime movers of information system projects. In the most successful companies, top management not only encouraged MIS indirectly by fostering a favorable, innovating atmosphere and inquiring approach, but also specifically spelled out the corporate commitment to the computer effort, its objectives, and operating management's responsibility for achieving the anticipated return.

Considerable research on the impact of perceptions of management support on the success of MIS has been carried out by Lucas.[10] He hypothesized a mechanism whereby high levels of management support and participation are translated into effective MIS; a high level of management involvement promotes favorable attitudes and perceptions of information service staff toward their jobs and towards users. Similarly, it promotes favorable attitudes and perceptions of users toward information systems and information system staff. In a field study of six companies, Lucas found positive relationships between perceived management support, perceived computer potential, and attitudes toward the EDP staff.[11] In another study he found that high levels of information sytem use (our criterion of success) are predicted by perceptions of high level management support together with positive evaluations of computer potential and positive attitudes toward computer output.

Lucas also formulates practical steps for management based on the relationship between perceptions of management support and MIS success.

For a manager to demonstrate support, he must reward and encourage the activities of the computer group leading to the development and operation of successful systems. . . . The manager must show by both his actions and own commitment of time to computer activities that he supports further use of the computer in the organization.[12]

Some rewards that might provide the necessary encouragement are letting user reactions influence raises and promotions for information system people and conditioning similar rewards for users on their participation in system development and use. Lucas also suggests that appointing a high-level steering committee composed of top managers and the data processing manager will demonstrate management support.

The responsibility of the MIS manager with respect to organizational perceptions is to act as a trigger to top management action. The information systems staff must inform management of the need for its involvement, initiate requests for active involvement, and make efforts to ensure that the involvement will be meaningful.

The various aspects of executive responsibility for MIS are summarized in table 5-1, which lists the relevant factors and suggests appropriate courses of action in each area.

Table 5-1
Summary of Executive Responsibility for MIS

Variables	Conclusions
Location and rank	The executive responsible for MIS should not be located in a specific functional area and should be no more than two levels below the chief officer of the organization.
	The rank of the responsible executive should be adapted to the stage of development of the MIS.
Association	Top management association with the MIS is highly conducive to success. Techniques for achieving executive involvement include the milestone approach to system development, incremental development plans, and the employment of outside consultants.
	Positive involvement of top management is not absolutely essential for success, nor is it sufficient to ensure success.
	Detachment of top management is caused by lack of understanding, lack of appreciation, and perceived threats to status.
Management functions and management time	Management should adapt its involvement in MIS to the stages of development and must devote sufficient time to performing the functions required in each stage.
Management functions and skills	The responsible executive needs strong administrative skills and a knowledge of computer technology. He should be a generalist with a system-oriented approach.
Organizational perceptions	A high level of top management involvement must be perceived in the organization. To achieve such organizational perception, management should reward both information and operations people involved in successful system development.
	The appointment of a high-level steering committee also increases organizational awareness of management support. The information systems manager should initiate managerial action indicative of management support.

Notes

1. Richard L. Nolan, "Managing the Computer Resource: A Stage Hypothesis," *Communications of the ACM*, vol. 16, no. 7 (July 1973), pp. 399-405.
2. Terrance Hanold, "An Executive View of MIS," *Datamation*, vol. 18, no. 11 (November 1972), pp. 65-71. Reprinted with the permission of DATAMATION® Copyright 1972 by Technical Publishing Company, Greenwich, Connecticut 06830.
3. John Dearden, "MIS is a Mirage," *Harvard Business Review*, vol. 51, no. 6 (January-February 1972), pp. 90-99.
4. E. Burton Swanson, "Management Information Systems: Appreciation and Involvement," *Management Science*, vol. 21, no. 2 (October 1974), pp. 178-188.
5. Richard L. Nolan, "Computer Data Base: The Future is Now." *Harvard Business Review*, vol. 51, no. 5 (September-October 1973), pp. 98-114.
6. John T. Garrity, "Top Management and Computer Profits," *Harvard Business Review*, vol. 41, no. 4 (July-August 1963), pp. 6-12, 172-174.
7. Tom Alexander, "Computers Can't Solve Everything," *Fortune*, vol. 80, no. 5 (October 1969), pp. 126 ff.
8. Kenneth R. MacCrimmon, "Descriptive Aspects of Team Theory: Observation, Communication and Decision Heuristics in Information Systems," *Management Science*, vol. 20, no. 10 (June 1974), pp. 1323-34.
9. Garrity, "Top Management and Computer Profits."
10. Henry C. Lucas, Jr., "A Descriptive Model of Information Systems in the Context of the Organization," *Data Base*, vol. 5, nos. 2, 3, and 4 (Winter 1973), pp. 27-39.
11. Henry C. Lucas, Jr., "Measuring Employee Reactions to Computer Operations." *Sloan Management Review*, vol. 15, no. 3 (Spring 1974), pp. 59-67.
12. Ibid.

Suggested Readings

Garrity, John T. "Top Management and Computer Profits." *Harvard Business Review*, vol. 41, no. 4 (July-August 1963), pp. 6-12, 172-174.
Hammond, John S., III, 'Do's and Don't's of Computer Models for Planning." *Harvard Business Review*, vol. 52, no. 2 (March-April 1974), pp. 110-123.
Lucas, Henry C., Jr. "Measuring Employee Reactions to Computer Operations." *Sloan Management Review*, vol. 15, no. 3 (Spring 1974), pp. 59-67.

MacCrimmon, Kenneth R. "Descriptive Aspects of Team Theory: Observation, Communication and Decision Heuristics in Information Systems." *Management Science*, vol. 20, no. 10 (June 1974), pp. 1323-34.

Nolan, Richard L. "Managing the Computer Resource: A Stage Hypothesis." *Communications of the ACM*, vol. 16, no. 7 (July 1973), pp. 399-405.

Swanson, E. Burton. "Management Information Systems: Appreciation and Involvement." *Management Science*, vol. 21, no. 2 (October 1974), pp. 178-188.

6   System Implementors

The second group of people involved in MIS—the system implementors—are discussed in this chapter. These information system professionals manage and execute the design, construction, and operation of MIS. Because the history of professional jobs in data processing is brief, standard job titles and job contents are only now beginning to appear. The Data Processing Management Association (DPMA) has pioneered the definition of such standards and accreditation of data processing personnel.

Prior to 1975, DPMA had administered examinations for a Certificate in Data Processing. In 1974, several professional societies, including DPMA and the Association for Computing Machinery (ACM), established the Institute for Certification of Computer Professionals (ICCP), which took over administration of the exams beginning in February 1975. Candidates for the Certificate must have at least 60 months experience in a computer-based information systems environment. The exam covers five areas: data-processing equipment, computer programming and software, principles of management, quantitative methods, and systems analysis and design. This development, however, is recent and has not yet had any great impact on the field.

In the absence of standards, overlapping job categories were developed in parallel in many organizations. Willoughby identified and analyzed fifty-six such tasks to arrive at seven job titles associated with data processing: supervisor, system project leader, system analyst, programmer, trainee, and other.[1] This and similar lists indicate that the three basic functional areas within the information systems profession are supervision, analysis, and programming.

In this chapter we discuss the variables of the groups of implementors that are relevant to their performance and to the success of MIS projects and MIS. The relevant variables are the roles, capabilities, recruitment, turnover, career paths, and rank of the implementors (see figure 6-1). Again, our scheme of presentation deals separately with MIS planning and implementation (chapters 3 and 4) and with each group participating in these stages. System implementors are but one of the groups participating, not the only one. Discussion of the interrelationships of the implementors with other groups, and indeed of interrelationships between all the groups, is deferred to chapter 8.

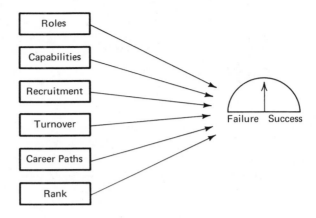

Figure 6-1. Implementors' Contributions to Success and Failure of Management Information Systems

Roles of System Implementors

Historically, goals for information systems were usually set by data-processing professionals. Today, however, the repeated recommendation is that executives, not implementors, should be responsible for goal definition. Understanding the reasons for this role shift aids an appreciation of the significance of the current recommendation.

Early information systems aimed for immediate effect on organizational profitability by direct reductions in costs or increases in revenues. Computer applications for achieving this aim (such as automation of clerical functions, inventory systems, or improved customer services) were easily identified and applied in similar ways in similar organizations. Goals were inherent to the area in which the computer was applied and effects on operating results were readily measurable. As applications became more sophisticated and assumed characteristics of MIS, they also became more dependent on the personality of the organization rather than on its area of business. Those who set the goals for MIS should understand the goals of the organization, its priorities, and the relevant opportunities and risks. All three are managerial rather than technological domains.

Gibson and Nolan view this development of the data-processing function over time as a stage process in which each stage poses different problems for management.[2] In the first two stages, because of a lack of formal guidelines for project selection, systems analysts tend to choose projects and set goals for them according to their own criteria such as past experience in other organizations, professional challenge, and ease of implementation, in addition to what they perceive to be the goals of the organization. Systems graduate to Stage 3 when managers replace systems implementors in defining goals. When this stage is reached, however, it is difficult to establish formal goal setting, which is accompanied by a reduction in power of those who previously set goals. Gibson and Nolan believe that the only way top management can recapture the goal-setting function is by enforcing replacement of high level computer personnel.

This relocation of goal setting can be difficult for both parties. For managers it entails the assumption of additional responsibilities that they are often not well qualified to assume; for implementors it entails the loss of considerable freedom of action. No matter how traumatic, the change is essential because poor choice of applications has often been traced back to a relegation of information system policy making to professionals. The chances of MIS success are enhanced if management knowledge of the business is applied to goal setting, and the more specifically the goals are defined, the greater the likelihood of success. (However, the obverse opinion has also been expressed, based on the belief that managers are incapable of knowing their requirements.[3] If this is the case in some organizations, implementors may be instrumental in suggesting potential goals; the final choice, however, should be managerial.)

Within the limits set by manager-dictated goals and users' requirements, implementors should have broad terms of reference. The role of the system implementor is to translate user needs into technically feasible system designs and to develop them on time and within budget. In our world of highly volatile computer technology, ever-innovative modes of application, and dynamic organizations, the MIS manager should have elbow room for design and implementation decisions. Thus decisions related to the MIS target are the responsibility of organizational executives, advised by implementors; decisions relating to the MIS project are the responsibility of implementors at the supervisory level.

Capabilities of System Implementors

The capabilities required of system implementors are considered in three sections—capabilities generally required of all implementation personnel, those required specifically of the supervisory level, and those specific to analysts and programmers.

General Capabilities

Breadth and depth of technical skills are the basis of implementor capabilities. Two surveys done about ten years apart found that a mastery of the technology differentiated successful from unsuccessful MIS efforts.[4] Interestingly, most studies on the capabilities of MIS implementors focus on such nontechnical capabilities as interpersonal skills and knowledge of management. This tendency may create the mistaken impression that technical capabilities are not important, but studies do not generally focus on technical skills because implementors now generally have formal training or at least supplementary courses and on-the-job training in data processing; as a result, one does not encounter situations in which these skills are entirely lacking. Most information units have trained people, some of them very good, others average or less. The differences between units are in the mix of good and average people, so that differentiations of overall skill levels are usually not very sharp. In addition, the possession of technical skills is so obvious a requirement as to leave little room for argument or need for verification.

Additional capabilities have been identified as essential for system implementors, beyond professional data-processing skills. These are concerned mainly with an understanding and appreciation of the organizational environment of the information system. Thus, implementors should have experience in the organization's operations to appreciate the issues involved. They also need a general knowledge of management processes and a specific understanding of the structure of management in their particular organization.

These capabilities may be summarized in the following list:

Training and talent, including design and programming talent

High competence and computer orientation

Experience in both the systems field and in the organization's operations

Knowledge of the processes of management

These capabilities are not specific to any one group of implementors, although different groups will require and use them in different degrees. The ensuing discussion will pinpoint more precisely the particular capabilities required of two major groups of implementors—supervisors (especially the information manager) and technicians (analysts and programmers).

Supervisors

In a controversial article, Dearden expressed the opinion that no one person can possess a broad enough set of skills required to implement an MIS (which he defined as a fully integrated total system).[5] This view is now generally accepted, even by opponents of Dearden's conclusions. The question then arises whether the chief implementor should possess primarily managerial skills or primarily technical ones.

A composite list of the capabilities required of information system managers, culled from a large number of opinions, includes the following characteristics:

The ability to command respect and confidence in the organization

The ability to obtain the cooperation of operating personnel

People-orientation, with an ability to act as motivator, educator, and change agent

Management skills, managing projects on time and within budget

Planning skills

Commitment to the goals of the organization

Political ability and experience

Salesmanship

A generalist, but technically oriented

Skill in modeling and using computers

This list was generated from opinions of practitioners as well as of academics and is based on personal experience and field studies. The exact wording is less important than the overall portrait—a manager, not a technician. True, professionalism is also important, but the weight assigned to managerial qualities overwhelms the references to technical skills. The answer to the question we posed at the beginning of this section is clear: managerial skills have primacy.

The general admonition to employ MIS chiefs who are good managers is correct, but incomplete. Not only should the top MIS executive be a good manager, but he should also have a personality that is consistent with the stage of development of the MIS organization. Morgan and Soden categorize MIS architects into five types labeled "flamboyant conceptualizer," "benign underachiever," "tyrant," "efficiency expert," and "fast tracker."[6]

These five types of MIS architects are differentiated in their ability to perform three management tasks—controlling, planning, and organizing. For example, the flamboyant conceptualizer tends to be strong on planning and organizing highly motivated young personnel, but weak on control and in organizing older, better established personnel. The tyrant, on the other hand, is strong on budgetary control and in organizing stable, veteran staff, but has no plan and does not motivate eager young personnel.

Nolan's much quoted model lists four stages of system development: (1) initiation, in which the system is first established; (2) contagion, when the information system concept takes hold in the organization and rapid development is demanded and undertaken; (3) control; and (4) integration.[7] During the contagion stage, the implementors are given free reign and tend to run loose, with projects getting out of control and winding up well beyond budget. When management realizes what has happened in the contagion stage, a renewed emphasis is placed on controls and appropriate procedures are introduced, formalized, and enforced. Once the new controls are established, the system enters a new stage of enhancing its effectiveness by integrating some of the many systems that were developed, somewhat haphazardly, during the contagion stage. Now, however, development projects are much more closely controlled and conform to some scheme of priorities.

Clearly, each stage of MIS maturity requires a different type of MIS architect. Thus the flamboyant conceptualizer is good during the contagion stage when he motivates an ambitious young staff to build projects on a broad front in conformance with some flamboyant scheme that he has conceptualized. This kind of regime will be impatient with the bottom lines of cost accounting and budgetary control. Next, a tyrant or efficiency expert is needed to bring things under control again. By now, the general principle should be clear; if MIS management is to remain effective, it must be periodically revised to accommodate the personality of the MIS chief to the degree of maturity of the MIS. Thus the replacement of MIS management is necessary not only when top management decides to set goals for the system, as described earlier; each time the organization's goals change as the MIS matures, it may be necessary to replace the old MIS chief with one more attuned to the current needs of the system. Some methods of reducing the traumas involved in such replacements are mentioned in the section on recruitment of MIS staff. (The need for such replacements is not the result of some natural law; the process of information system maturation and consequent incompatibility of the old MIS chief with the new level of maturity is an often observed empirical fact but is not inevitable. Some personality types, such as the efficiency expert and the fast tracker, may do a creditable job in all stages. Thus careful selection of the MIS chief in the early stages of system development may obviate the need for painful future readjustments. Furthermore, the organization may completely avoid periods of loss of control followed by stagnation.)

Analysts and Programmers

It is fairly general practice that programmers are eventually promoted to become systems analysts under the implicit assumption that both groups have similar capabilities. Gibson and Nolan, however, point out their basic differences.[8] Computer programmers are highly skilled and creative professionals, technologically oriented, with interests and motivation stemming from performance in their profession. The organizational climate means little to them because their professional peers are their primary reference group. The work of the systems analyst, on the other hand, is closely interwoven with the larger organization. They have to be in close interrelationships with users and operating management and are exposed to the mode of operation of the organization, as well as its goals and priorities. Because of these differences, there is no reason to assume that a good programmer will necessarily make a good analyst. In fact, as we will show shortly, the capabilities required of each of these professions is very different and there is reason to believe that good programmers will generally *not* make good analysts.

In addition to their basic technical knowledge and understanding of management processes, systems analysts should possess a broad set of desirable characteristics. Wofsey lists twenty-six such characteristics collected from seven works on the subject.[9] These characteristics, in descending order of the number of works relating to them, are logical ability, thoroughness, ability to work with others, resourcefulness, imagination, oral ability, abstract reasoning, emotional balance, interest in analysis, writing ability, curiosity, decisiveness, empathy, mature judgment, practicality, ability to observe, dislike of inefficiency, initiative, integrity, intelligence, interest in science and technology, interest in staff work, numerical ability, openmindedness, and selling ability.

Although no formal links have yet been established between analysts' capabilities and system success, this comprehensive list, supported by a high degree of agreement about the first five items, points to the nature of the analysts' work and the characteristics required of them—particularly an inquiring mind and the ability to relate detailed analyses to a comprehensive view of the total organizational picture.

Opinions of programmer characteristics are as unsupported as those of analysts. Many desirable personality traits for programmers have been listed. The Bureau of Labor Statistics has issued a list of programmer traits derived from studying sixteen organizations. The traits, listed in decreasing order of the number of organizations referring to them are understanding of underlying principles, report writing ability, responsibility for planning, adaptability to a variety of duties, judgment based on quantity, adaptability to precise standards, judgment based on quality, adaptation to deadline pressures, observation, rapid arithmetic, knowledge of accounting, knowledge of decimals and fractions, adaptability to repetitive operations, knowledge of calculus, knowledge of theoretical mathematics, rapid coordination, and rapid manipulation of small objects. No organizations listed the last two traits.

However, little evidence supports any of these conjectures and very little is known, in fact, of the personality sets conducive to good performance of MIS jobs. Such lists, however, may become a starting point for building a capabilities base within the organization. The organization should first decide which characteristics best fit its needs. What combination does it want of speed, economy, creativeness, obedience, independence, or a core for promotion to system analysts? Only after such decisions have been made can the organization identify the traits most suited to its needs and select its programmers accordingly. We feel that only a small percentage of programmers are always "good" or always "bad" programmers, regardless of the organizational context. The approach of an organization to its MIS results in specific kinds of systems with different capabilities required. Even within a single MIS unit, different tasks require different programmer specialties. Thus maintenance work on an existing system is different from work on a crash development program, which is again different from the work of the systems programmer who maintains the basic software packages such as the operating system and data base management systems.

Recruitment of MIS Staff

Obviously, staffing uncertainties are a major difficulty in managing MIS and a source of major errors. One rather extreme view states that all MIS failures are failures of MIS management and personnel.[10] We believe that top management as well as users share the responsibility for MIS success and failure, but that implementors and their skills are one of the critical ingredients of success. Furthermore, because top management delegates some of its responsibilities to the MIS executive, his recruitment and appointment is a major decision in MIS development.

For all three groups of implementors, the three basic decisions relate to recruitment inside or outside the organization, the method of selection, and professions or skill categories from which to recruit—that is, where, how, and whom to recruit.

Where?

The question whether to recruit insiders, with knowledge and experience of the organization, or outsiders with experience in MIS arises because surveys and personal experience show that both computer expertise and understanding business problems are necessary. Because both capabilities rarely occur in a single individual, two alternatives exist: to teach information technology to some of the organization's functional experts or to teach computer professionals the workings of the organization in sufficient depth. Each solution has, of course, its pros and cons.

For the MIS executive, an understanding of the organization overwhelms the importance of technical sophistication. Of course, technical skills are also relevant at this level, but many effective MIS executives have only a limited knowledge of the technology but complement it with a thorough understanding of the organization. Thus it is preferable, when possible, that the supervisory levels of the MIS unit be recruited from inside the organization; this possibility may be constrained, however, by considerations relating to the personality traits required at various stages of MIS development elaborated in the preceding section.

MIS executives may come from two internal sources. Either middle managers with strong administrative skills may be converted into MIS managers by education in computers and information systems; alternatively, senior systems analysts or project leaders, who have become well acquainted with the organization and have demonstrated a potential for management during their careers may be promoted. This second alternative has been especially recommended because it demonstrates to systems analysts and programmers that there are rewards to balancing professional interests with organizational needs.[11]

In supervisory jobs below the MIS director, such as senior systems analysts and project leaders, technical knowledge becomes relatively more important. Nevertheless, understanding organizational processes is mandatory for all supervisory staff and systems analysts. Again, people with line experience in the organization may be co-opted into systems development, but they will require considerable training in information systems before becoming effective as project leaders; the amount of technical expertise required at this level is much greater than for the MIS chief.

The advantages of in-house recruitment of all three groups of MIS implementors are quite considerable; they include a knowledge of the organization on the part of the candidate, an acquaintance of the candidate and his abilities on the part of the organization, low turnover, and lower salary costs. Another significant advantage of internal recruitment is to provide a career path into well-paid jobs for clerical personnel in the organization, who may be antagonized when they see many good jobs going to outsiders. Among its disadvantages are the probable lack of technical skills within the organization and consequent high cost of training in data processing, a lower tendency of people who do not see themselves primarily as information professionals to innovate and keep abreast of the state of the art, and finally the quality of people that other departments are willing to release.

Outside sources are MIS personnel in other organizations and consulting firms. The high turnover among MIS professionals, to be discussed in a later section, makes for a lively market in this kind of labor. Systems analysts, unlike programmers, are experts in a limited number of areas and their skills may be relevant to only a few functions, organizations, or industries. However, there are people on the market with experience in almost every industry and function who possess the technical skills and most of the organizational understanding needed by any organization.

Because their skills are more universal and less specific to any one kind of organization, programmers require less adaptation in moving from one firm to another, but may need to convert from one kind of machine to another or from one programming language to a different one. Staff hired from consulting firms are especially useful for handling temporary surges in development work and may also have the benefit of previous exposure to many different organizations, or even knowledge of the specific organization through previous consulting work. However, the use of outside consultants in not very extensive and is discussed in more detail in chapter 4.

In most cases, organizations do not recruit entirely from one source, but usually tap a number of sources. To solve its MIS recruitment problem optimally, an organization will usually need people from both inside and outside the organization to get the best fit of skills to its needs. In many cases, it will be impossible to recruit exactly the mix of skills and experience wanted because of the constraints imposed by the availability of the various characteristics that make up the mix. Recruitment should start, however, with a clear policy about the desired makeup of manpower and then proceed to fit such goals as closely as possible.

How?

Testing is widely used in selecting analysts and programmers, especially the latter. To appraise data-processing personnel such tests are used as programmer aptitude tests (PAT, RPAT, ATPP), the Wonderlic Personnel Test, the Computer Programmer Aptitude Battery, the Watson-Glaser Critical Thinking Appraisal, interest tests, and personality tests.[12] Validation studies of these tests are somewhat disappointing. Like similar tests in other professions, test results are moderately correlated with college or university grades and show low correlations with supervisors' performance ratings. One finding is clear—intelligent people make good programmers. Although there are as yet no proven tools for selecting data-processing personnel, each organization may employ those tests which best fit its requirements. Experimentation will probably turn up one or two tests that perform reasonably well in the specific environment.

In selecting MIS executives the situation is even worse. As in many other areas, selection of the supervisory level is based on judgment. The key contribution of top management to MIS development, the screening of candidates for executive positions, however, is usually performed very ineffectively. In their study of MIS failure, Morgan and Soden state that "the key factor for success of anyone in the MIS area is the ability to write good resumes."[13]

Apparently it is difficult for judgment to penetrate the façade of a good resume. Recruiting executives from within the organization, whether managers in other areas or senior MIS personnel, reduces the uncertainty involved in selecting outsiders and enables management to use general organizational criteria for promotion to executive positions. Our previous discussion of the capabilities required of MIS executives also favors internal recruitment where possible. When the appropriate person is not available internally, however, there is no choice but to recruit externally with all the attendant uncertainty. When this situation arises, the best solution is, again, to define as clearly as possible the characteristics required and to select the candidate closest to that definition.

Who?

The elements of the recruitment decision should be complemented by an additional consideration—the professional backgrounds that should be represented in the implementation group. The four relevant professional groups are computer and data-processing professionals, operations research professionals, people with experience in the organization, and people sensitive to the significance and effects of organizational change.

The core of the implementation staff is, of course, a body of information-processing professionals, recruited either internally or externally on the basis of their technical competence. Surveys show that reinforcement of this core staff by management science professionals promotes MIS success. These people are trained to think in terms of optimization—that is, doing the best job possible under the circumstances and with the available resources—rather than in terms of technological imperatives disregarding cost. It may be difficult to find personnel inside the organization with operations research skills and the desire to be trained in data processing. This combination, however, is now quite common in university programs; most programs in information systems require at least an introduction to operations research; many also require advanced work.

Line managers, preferably potential users, are a third necessary ingredient in project development teams. These people think in terms of the organization and its processes; because MIS are developed for a specific organization, the organizational view must complement technical know-how at all levels of the development team.

The fourth professional skill is sensitivity to the problems of change in organizations. Organizational development and change is studied and taught in programs in organizational behavior. This field, usually too "soft" for technically oriented people, deals with the introduction of changes into organizations and their effects on human commitment and alienation during and after the process. Because the introduction of MIS involves considerable changes in the organization and its methods of operation, including personnel with this background may help to avoid some problems and to alleviate those which are unavoidable. It is their responsibility to increase the acceptability of the new systems, thereby increasing their use.

Most people possess only one of these sets of skills and others possess two, but it is unrealistic to expect any single person to be proficient in all four areas (in any case, we have never encountered such a paragon). Thus, in practice, mixed teams are used. Many of the conflicts which arise between implementors and users (discussed at length in chapter 8) are internalized by such mixed teams. Once the implementation team reaches consensus, problems in application and use should be greatly reduced.

Ideally, the MIS executive should possess all four skill sets but obviously this requirement is infeasible. Because the MIS executive, however, is first and foremost a manager, the particular professional background from which he was elevated to his executive position is secondary to his managerial skills. If his knowledge of the technology is sufficient, if he can understand and weight the relative importance of the arguments of each skill area, and, above all, if he has well-developed managerial skills, he has the potential required for managing the MIS function.

Turnover of MIS Staff

In recruiting new personnel there are costs involved in candidate searches, selection, training, placement, and follow-up. These initial costs are considerable and are increasing in the higher positions. Such costs, as a matter of fact, are investments in human capital expected to bear fruit during the employee's service in the organization. Over the last decade, more attention has been paid to this investment as part of the efforts toward better management practices. A high rate of turnover means that part of the investment is lost; no turnover, on the other hand, leads to stagnation. Because it is difficult to measure employee contributions, it is also difficult to calculate the optimal rate of turnover for each job and organization. A surrogate for good turnover rates is the practice in other organizations or industries or similar jobs in other functions in the same organization.

Willoughby found that MIS people are characterized by turnover rates of 15 to 20 percent, about the same as for other professions staffed by young people with few years of service.[14] He concludes that this rate of turnover is not excessive. We are not really interested, however, in the absolute rate, but in the effect that turnover has on system development. On this point most observers agree that the development of systems has suffered from the rates of turnover. In these terms, the rate of turnover is very high. Furthermore, within these average rates, some organizations exhibit much higher rates of turnover than others. In such organizations, turnover may contribute to delays in implementing systems, high costs, and system failure.

High rates of turnover result from ineffective selection processes, faulty methods of introducing new employees into the organization, dissatisfaction among the information services staff, organizational pressures (mainly from users), lack of career paths (a particularly important issue dealt with in the next section), and, of course, opportunities in other organizations promising higher ranks and salaries. An organization suffering from excessive turnover must identify and mitigate the reasons for it. Exit interviews and postexit questionnaires are good ways of identifying these reasons.

However, reducing turnover for its own sake is not recommended. Information should be gathered and analyzed about turnover rates in other organizations. Efforts to achieve much lower rates than the average are both expensive and ineffective and may even be detrimental to the organization. Only when all the relevant information is in hand and has been studied should a decision be made about goals for the rate of turnover among information system staff.

Career Paths

A major organizational problem in information system staff that has not yet been satisfactorily solved is career paths. This problem affects each group of system implementors; our discussion will focus on each in turn.

Programmers

As we mentioned earlier, the usual solution for programmer career paths is to promote veteran programmers to be systems analysts. The two jobs, however, have almost diametrically opposed requirements. The programmer is trained to take infinite pains with detail, never sees the complete organization, rarely sees a complete information system, and in some cases may not even see a complete program. The systems analyst, on the other hand, while dealing with detail, must also see the organization as a whole and the intermeshing of its subsystems—especially when a top-down approach is adopted. Promotion of veteran programmers who have been taught to think detail into systems analysts who are supposed to think broad-brush very often turns a good programmer into a poor and frustrated systems analyst. In some cases, promotion to chief programmer or consultant to junior programmers is a partial solution. The much higher salaries usually commanded by systems analysts, however, drive programmers in that direction. Apparently, the best solution is to provide special titles and increased salaries for senior programmers, even though their job content may not be very different from their junior peers. This solution may seem to be expensive, but it is probably cheaper than keeping ineffective and poorly qualified systems analysts. The precise solution, however, must depend on the particular organization and its possibilities. In some cases there may be no alternative but to encourage senior programmers to leave or to transfer into unrelated jobs in the organization so that they can be replaced by junior people for whom there is still room for development.

Systems Analysts

The outlook for systems analysts is somewhat better than for programmers, because they may become project leaders, acquire managerial skills, and become MIS executives. Such promotions, however, can solve the problem for only a small minority, and for an especially gifted minority at that. One solution for prolonging the service of systems analysts in the organization is to provide them with tours of duty in functional areas where they may see things from a different point of view, thus broadening their perspectives and renewing their interest.

In the long run, however, those analysts without managerial talent almost inevitably feel that their advancement is blocked, as indeed it is, and will be drawn to some other organization that offers new challenges and more pay for their particular set of skills. It is not good for an organization to keep the same systems analysts for too long because they lose their creativity and innovativeness after a long period in the same environment. Thus using migration into other fields in the organization may be the best solution of the systems analyst's career path problem.

Supervisors

The career path problem is probably least severe for MIS executives. We have already pointed out that the personality of the MIS chief should be adapted to the stage of information system maturity, which usually implies a change in management from one stage to the next. Top management as well as MIS managers tend to think in terms of three-year contracts for the position.[15] This practice was established mainly because the generally abrasive relationship between MIS managers and users tends to erode MIS managers. These reasons, together with the general need for a periodic change in outlook and for new approaches, all point to the desirability of a fairly rapid turnover rate among MIS executives.

Because MIS managers should be chosen primarily for their managerial ability, not for their technical sophistication, their turnover should not create real problems either for them or for the organization. If they are indeed good managers, they will generally be very happy to resume their advancement in a functional area other than MIS. Because good managers are a commodity always in short supply, the organization will also be happy to employ them in some other area where their talents will do most good.

Hayes and Nolan present a scenario for MIS executive development that is consistent with our analysis and that may also be a partial solution to the career path problem for systems analysts.[16] They picture a young person who joins the organization, works for several years in line positions, and then has a managerial job in a functional area. Next he is sent to a management development program that includes instruction in computers and planning. On returning to the organization, this person is temporarily assigned to a group involved in developing MIS in the functional area with which he is familiar. Thus, this person has the required capabilities, regards the job as part of his career path, and stays in that job for only a limited time. Such a person will be an excellent candidate at a later point in his career to be MIS manager. This scenario points out that the solution to management career paths in MIS is not to regard the information system as a closed function with its own career paths, but rather as a normal station on the career paths of managers from any area in the organization.

Rank

The rank of the MIS manager is at least a partial indication of the importance of the MIS to the organization and of the ability of the implementors to command respect and to act effectively. In chapter 5 we pointed out that the executive responsible for MIS should be no more than two hierarchical levels below the general manager of the organization for adequate status. Naturally, the MIS director should report to this executive. A gradual increase in the status of the MIS director accompanies the maturation of MIS; eventually, the post of MIS director graduates to the ranks of senior management at the vice-president level or its equivalent. In these cases, executive responsibility and MIS management become embodied in one position.

The variables related to implementors of MIS are summarized in Table 6-1.

Table 6-1
Summary of Implementor Variables in MIS

Variables	Conclusions
Roles of implementors	Goals should be set by management, not by implementors.
	Within managerially defined goals, implementors should be given responsibility and authority for design and implementation.
Capabilities of implementors	General capabilities: all implementation personnel should be technically proficient, should have experience in both information systems and the organization's operations and should understand the management processes of the organization.
	Supervisors: MIS executives should be primarily good managers and their style of management should be compatible with the stage of development of information systems in the organization.
	Analysts and programmers: analysts should be inquiring by nature and should have the ability to relate detailed analyses to the overall organizational picture. Programmers should be technologically oriented and should be appointed to the kind of programming task best suited to their skills.
Recruitment of MIS staff	Recruiting MIS staff from people inside the organization who already understand the organization processes has considerable advantages.
	To get the best mix of skills, organizations usually recruit some of their MIS staff internally and some externally.
	Great difficulties are encountered in effectively selecting MIS chiefs.
	Tests are available for technical MIS staff, but their results show low correlations with supervisors' performance ratings.
	The MIS implementation group requires skills in information processing, operations research, organizational processes, and managing organizational change. To achieve this set of skills in development teams it is necessary to mix people of different backgrounds.
Turnover rates	Turnover rates for MIS personnel tend to be high. Realistic goals for turnover rates prevent excessive costs and stagnation on one hand and prevent serious disruptions on the other.

Table 6-1 (cont.)

Career paths	Programmers rarely make good systems analysts and career paths for programmers should lead into senior programming appointments or into other careers in the organization.
	Systems analysts tend to be organizationally oriented and their career paths should include tours of duty in functional areas and even into general management.
	Because the principal requirement of MIS supervisors is that they be good managers, MIS supervision should be a station on the career paths of managers from all areas of the organization.
Rank	To assure adequate status, the MIS supervisor should be two or three levels below the chief executive.

Notes

1. Theodore C. Willoughby, "Staffing the MIS Function," *Computing Surveys,* vol. 4, no. 4 (December 1972), pp. 241-259.

2. Cyrus F. Gibson and Richard L. Nolan, "Managing the Four Stages of EDP Growth," *Harvard Business Review,* vol. 52, no. 1 (January-February 1974), pp. 76-88.

3. Russel L. Ackoff, "Management Misinformation Systems," *Management Science,* vol. 14, no. 4 (December 1967), pp. 147-156.

4. John T. Garrity, "Top Management and Computer Profits," *Harvard Business Review,* vol. 41, no. 4 (July-August 1963), pp. 6-12, 172-174. See also Kent W. Colton, "Computers and Police: Patterns of Success and Failure," *Sloan Management Review,* vol. 14, no. 2 (Winter 1972-73), pp. 75-97.

5. John Dearden, "MIS Is a Mirage," *Harvard Business Review,* vol. 50, no. 1 (January-February 1972), pp. 90-99.

6. Howard L. Morgan and John V. Soden, "Understanding MIS Failures," *Data Base,* vol. 5, nos. 2, 3, and 4 (Winter 1973), pp. 157-171.

7. Richard L. Nolan, "Managing the Computer Resource: A Stage Hypothesis," *Communications of the ACM,* vol. 16, no. 7 (July 1973), pp. 399-405.

8. Gibson and Nolan, "Managing the Four Stages of EDP Growth."

9. Marvin M. Wofsey, *Management of Automatic Data Processing* (Washington D.C.: Thompson, 1968).

10. Morgan and Soden, "Understanding MIS Failures."

11. Gibson and Nolan, "Managing the Four Stages of EDP Growth."

12. Willoughby, "Staffing the MIS Function."

13. Morgan and Soden, "Understanding MIS Failures."

130

14. Willoughby, "Staffing the MIS Function."
15. Gibson and Nolan, "Managing the Four Stages of EDP Growth."
16. Robert H. Hayes and Richard L. Nolan, "What Kind of Corporate Modeling Functions Best," *Harvard Business Review,* vol. 52, no. 3 (May-June 1974), pp. 102-112.

Suggested Readings

Brill, Alan E. "The Alienation of the Systems Analyst." *Journal of Systems Management,* vol. 25, no. 1 (January 1974), pp. 26-29.
Colton, Kent W. "Computers and Police: Patterns of Success and Failure." *Sloan Management Review,* vol. 14, no. 2 (Winter 1972-73), pp. 75-97.
Morgan, Howard L., and Soden, John V. "Understanding MIS Failures." *Data Base,* vol. 5, nos. 2, 3, and 4 (Winter 1973), pp. 157-171.
Willoughby, Theodore C. "Staffing the MIS Function." *Computing Surveys,* vol. 4, no. 4 (December 1972), pp. 241-259.

7 Users of MIS

In the last two chapters we discussed two of the three groups of actors taking part in the design, implementation, and operation of MIS—top management and system implementors. In this chapter we will discuss the third group—users of MIS. The users of a management information system are those managers in the organization to whom the outputs of the system are directed for decision-making purposes. This definition excludes members of the organization who may come into contact with the MIS, but do not use it to make decisions. Clerical or other operating personnel who receive outputs for operational purposes do not come under this definition, nor do the people who prepare data or feed them to the system.

The great importance of the users as an integral part of any system that purports to be an MIS is implicit in our definition in chapter 1:

A management information system is a system . . . *which is used*, or desired, by one or more managers. . . .

In the absence of use, or desire for use, by managers, an information system cannot claim the title of MIS, no matter what the intent of its designers. Because we also defined the success of a system in terms of the extent of its use, the users clearly become a critical element in the system and a vital contributor to success or failure. It is therefore important to understand how users interface with the system, especially because this interface is by no means simple or troublefree; neither will it somehow take care of itself.

The discussion in this chapter divides the factors affecting users into two main groups. The first group includes the variables that can be considered in relative isolation from each other: user requirements, user rank, user capabilities, user motivation, and cognitive styles of users. These variables may be thought of as directly affecting MIS success. The remaining variables—prior attitudes of users, user involvement, user education, and change resistance—form a rather complex system that must be dealt with as a whole (see figure 7-1). A last variable—the user-implementor relationship and the conflict inherent in it—is briefly mentioned here and elaborated on in chapter 8.

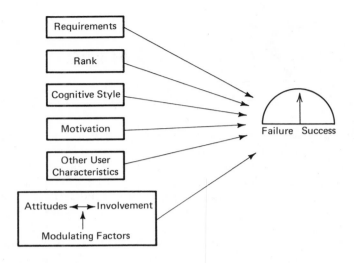

Figure 7-1. User Contributions to Success and Failure of Management Information Systems

User Requirements

Specifications for an MIS project, discussed in chapter 4, are an operationalization of the goals of the system, the end product of the planning phase, and the first stage of the project implementation phase. User requirements, the topic of this section, are related but not identical to system specifications. User requirements are the information needed by the user in fulfilling his managerial tasks, expressed in terms of the content, scope, quality, accuracy, and timeliness of the information required. These requirements may be translated, directly or after modification, into specifications for the construction of management information systems.

Virtually all recipes for the construction of MIS take it for granted that user requirements can be accurately identified in advance. Although even this basic assumption will be examined later, we can accept it at this stage for the sake of clarity. Under this assumption, there are two basic and contradictory approaches to defining the information needs of users. The first approach is to simply *ask* users what their requirements are. The second approach denies the effectiveness of letting users define their requirements and states that the implementor must employ his expertise to *tell* managers what information they need.

In practice, simply asking managers to define their information needs is extremely inefficient and ineffective because managers can rarely state such needs with any degree of precision. Several methods have been suggested for overcoming this difficulty. One method is to consult several users whose needs would appear to be identical—branch managers of a bank or of a retail chain, for example. When such consensus planning is infeasible, another possible method to identify managers' needs is to present them with initial models, or prototypes, suggested by the expert's analysis. Of course both methods can be used in parallel.

Asking managers about their information needs is sometimes recommended as a method of establishing communications between users and implementors and so motivating use of the system. However, in addition to the objective inability to state requirements that is often encountered, managers frequently feel threatened by information system development and by the "prying" of the analyst into their former preserves. In such cases, managers may make omissions, they may exaggerate, or they may be inaccurate, vague, or nonspecific.

A first step away from relying on users' statements and toward telling managers what their needs are is for the expert to analyze managers' current information. This approach implies that although the manager may be incapable when interviewed of imparting his needs, observing his behavior will reveal what those needs are. Analyzing current information use is not a very ambitious approach: it results in the legitimization and automation of existing practices. Thus the expert employing this approach is interested in the information that currently reaches the manager, not in how the manager uses the information. Later, when the same information is supplied by an MIS, modifications may be made—information may be added or condensed and report frequencies may be changed. The information used is analyzed, not the decisions made. In this approach, the system implementors act as technicians rather than as experts.

The merit of the information analysis approach is its acceptability. Managers already accustomed to manual information systems receive the same information, but in the form of computer output rather than conventional reports. No changes in habit or decision-making procedures are necessary. The shortcomings are also clear; rather than using MIS as a lever to improve management methods, practices are duplicated that were developed when better information was inaccessible, too expensive, or too time-consuming.

Naturally, most writers who discuss the use of expertise to define information requirements refer to decision analysis rather than to the analysis of current information. The experts' task in this case is to (1) isolate the nature, frequency, and interrelationships of the major decisions in the organization; (2) identify the managers by whom the decisions are made; and (3) then determine what information is needed for the decisions and to define the required characteristics of that information. Ackoff argues an extreme statement of the case for this approach based on the premise that even with the best of intentions, managers are incapable of accurately determining their own information needs.[1]

The expertise required for a decision-information analysis includes expertise in management practice as well as in information systems. One proponent of this approach views the analysis of managerial information as an integral part of the field of organization theory.[2] Thus the analyst should ask what the manager does. He then prescribes how best to do it and identifies the information needed to perform in this best way, including detailed examples to show that his approach is feasible. Hax, who sets universal guidelines for planning an MIS for a manufacturing and distributing company, proposes a similar approach.[3] He recommends analyzing functional, departmental, and product information requirements based on the way such a company *should* be managed.

In short, this method is analogous to the classic time and motion study approach but applied to managers rather than to manipulative or clerical employees. Because managerial jobs are concerned with decision making rather than operations, the focus of the study is shifted from finding the best ways to handle materials, perform operations, or route forms to finding the best way to make decisions and the information inputs needed to make such decisions. Zani has operationalized this approach by suggesting a series of questions the decision analyst should ask: "What decisions are made? What decisions need to be made? What factors are important in making these decisions? How and when should these decisions be made? What information is useful in making these decisions?"[4] This set of questions could be used as a checklist by an expert making his analysis from first principles, or they could be put to managers. Which brings us full circle and returns us to the method of asking managers what their needs are.

Each approach to information analysis that we have mentioned has its proponents. Those at the "ask them what they need" end of the spectrum argue that their method is the best way to achieve user involvement and eventual use. Those at the other extreme—the "tell them what they need" approach—claim that few managers know what information they need and that they do not need the information they want. As in many such arguments, we feel the best solution lies in the middle between the extremes. Good system definitions result from an effort by the system designer both to understand the decision problem thoroughly and to extract as much information and intuition as possible from the users while actively involving them in the analysis.

Evidence that users' information needs can be identified in advance is not always consistent. In at least one organization, the ability to define user needs for each level of management was a basic assumption underlying a successful development program and was incorporated in the organization's definition of MIS: "We define a management information system as one in which the requirements at each level of management are carefully determined in advance of need. . . ."[5]

On the other hand, there are reports of cases in which major efforts to identify information needs in advance were at best incomplete. In a Department of Defense research and development information system "No amount of systems analysis, O.R., method studies, or direct interrogation would have ever detected the need for some of the questions that have been asked in the first year of operation."[6]

The higher up in the organizational hierarchy, the more nonrecurring and the more unstructured decisions are. Such decisions make it even more difficult to predefine the nature of the decision process and more futile to attempt to define information needs in advance. At the highest levels, decisions are often not amenable to either modeling or algorithmic solutions, and the managers involved are often incapable of even defining the information they want or the criteria they will use.

Decision making in the higher echelons becomes more sophisticated as the managers acquire experience and changes in scope as the nature of the job evolves and areas of responsibility are redefined. Thus even if the nature of decision making at this level is captured at some time, the information system developed for it over a year or two will be obsolete by the time it is completed. In these cases information analysis seems to be the better alternative—trying to make available as much information as may conceivably be useful while foregoing attempts to grasp the particular decision situations. In these cases, systems should be oriented toward flexibility, evolution in parallel with the decisions required, and ad hoc modeling or simulation of contingencies rather than prior programming.

Rank

The rank variable deals with the effects of the rank of the managers on their behavior as users. There are, as yet, no reports of direct use of MIS by chief executive officers. Various surveys of executive use of computerized information systems all reach the same conclusion: direct use of MIS by chief executives either via direct access terminals or through computer outputs is nonexistent.

The question raised is whether this lack of use of MIS at the top is a result of the nature of the decision problem at that level or whether it is a result of some defect in management that should be remedied. The answer seems to be that, at least in part, the nature of the decision problem prohibits direct top management use of MIS.

Brady's model of top management decision making has five basic steps: identification of a decision situation, analysis of the situation, formulation of alternative courses of action, evaluation of the alternatives, and selection of a course of action.[7] In which of these steps could computers aid top management? Theoretically, MIS could be designed for each stage. But because of the unstructured and political nature of top management decision making, because of the intuitive nature of chief executives, and because of the way in which decision criteria tend to shift during the fairly long decision cycle at this level, it seems that in practice, MIS can be of real assistance in only three of the five phases—identification, analysis, and evaluation. It does not seem likely that the formulation and selection of alternatives will be trusted to information systems in the near future. Thus the essential needs of decision making—formulating and selecting alternatives—are not met at the highest levels and must explain at least some of the lack of use of MIS by the highest executives.

Those aspects of top management decision making which can be assisted by MIS—identification, analysis, and evaluation—are typically delegated by top executives to subordinates. Thus middle management participates in top management decision making. In fulfilling its role in the decision process, middle management can and does make use of MIS. Top management is presented with reports and recommendations that incorporate or are based on MIS outputs. Thus, the benefits of MIS are made available to top executives who become indirect users of the systems and whose decision making may be improved as a result of the better staff work done for them.

Though the direct use of MIS by chief executives is as yet unknown, such use has filtered up from the lower echelons as far as the vice-presidential level. Typically, young MBAs with some training in the technology who have risen rapidly in their organizations have introduced MIS into those organizations and use them themselves. In the foreseeable future, this new generation of managers will probably accede to the executive suit; along with them, the use of computerized information systems will also rise into the highest levels and become corporationwide.

It is possible that the level of management using MIS directly is an indication of success, but it is important to take into account the nature of top management decision making and its constraints on the use of MIS. The target is often stated by both top executives and implementors of having the chief executive manage the organization through a terminal in his office. This view of the top executive's task is somewhat mechanistic and a somewhat naive evaluation of the state of the art of both management and MIS technologies. When these technologies and their potential users are sufficiently mature, the terminals will naturally find their way into the executive suite and the boardroom. Forcing the terminal into those regions will not make the technology suddenly appear, nor will it alter deeply rooted decision habits.

Cognitive Styles of Users

The interaction of the cognitive styles of users with the output of an information system has significant bearing on its success. Considerable evidence on the mechanics of this interaction is available in the empirical studies and conclusions of McKenney and Keen on which we draw heavily in this section.[8] The communications gap between managers and management scientists triggered their series of studies on interpersonal differences in cognitive styles. Cognitive style, the way people think and solve problems, was decomposed by McKenney and Keen into two dimensions, following Jungian psychology; these two dimensions are information gathering and information evaluation.

Along the information-gathering dimension, individuals tend to be either *preceptive* or *receptive*. Preceptive individuals filter incoming data according to their prior concepts and tend to perceive *gestalts* or whole pictures. Receptive individuals are sensitive to bits of data independently of their conceptual frameworks. Thus, the more receptive people are attentive to details, look for complete data sets, and avoid preconceptions; those who are more preceptive look for cues, relationships in the data, and extract parts of the data to create new combinations and precepts.

The information evaluation or problem-solving dimension is related to the sequence in which the data that have been gathered are then analyzed. On this dimension, individuals who are basically *systematic* look for a method that, when used, will guarantee the best solution. Individuals who are more *intuitive* thinkers do not commit themselves to any particular method; they may try and retry many different approaches in a trial-and-error fashion. Intuitive thinkers tend to redefine a problem frequently, relate to the total problem rather than to its component parts, jump backward and forward in the process of analysis, and simultaneously formulate, evaluate, and abandon alternatives in rapid succession; systematic thinkers look for an approach and a method and advance through the problem-solving process in an orderly sequential fashion.

Cognitive style, then, is the location of the individual in the two-dimensional space formed by the styles of information gathering and information analysis. Problem-solvers may be receptive-systematic, receptive-intuitive, preceptive-systematic or preceptive-intuitive; usually they are somewhere along each of the dimensions and not necessarily at the theoretical extremes. Thus, different people have different cognitive styles—not better or worse but different. Furthermore, McKenney and Keen found that there are categories of problems (and careers) to which some cognitive styles are better fitted, while opposite cognitive styles are more compatible with other problems and careers. To quote their examples: auditor and clinical diagnostician are roles especially compatible with the receptive-systematic cognitive style; architect and bond salesman with receptive-intuitive; marketing manager, psychologist, and historian with preceptive-intuitive; and production and logistics manager, statistician, and financial analyst with preceptive-systematic.

Every information system produces information in a certain way; content, style of presentation, level of aggregation, format, and method of presentation are either predetermined or limited within fairly narrow bounds. These bounds are compatible with a certain range of cognitive styles in users. If the user happens to be within this range, he will probably use the system. If the system produces information that is alien to the cognitive style of the potential user, it is very unlikely that he will use it.

Because their decision-making style is highly intuitive, very personal, and informal, top managers tend to be preceptive-intuitive or possibly receptive-intuitive. If they are to accommodate the needs of such managers, systems must be able to cater to individual requests. Rather than producing standard, structured outputs, or being based on a single rigid model, they should be able to present data in different ways, answer "what if" questions, permit changes in assumptions, and provide for intuitive and judgmental inputs; such systems should enable problems to be illuminated from different angles rather than presenting pat solutions.

In practice, it is not even enough to place an individually adaptable system at the user's disposal. Users often believe that they must adjust themselves to the information system and expect to be told exactly how to use it rather than telling the system what they want. It can be quite difficult, sometimes, to persuade users that they can determine the information they get in accordance with their needs. Thus, not only must the system be such that it can be tailored to individual needs, but managers must also perceive it as being so. Only when systems are built to adapt themselves to the individual needs of each manager and only when managers know how to define their needs to the system, should we expect to find a high level of information system use by top management directly.

Motivation

Assuming both that managers-users are totally oriented toward their task and that managers are very rational, it has been claimed that information systems, because they improve mangerial performance, will automatically motivate potential users to use them. Our discussion of cognitive styles should already have weakened this claim because an information system may improve the performance of some managers but not of others. In addition, some empirical evidence undermines this claim even further; it shows that even if a system does improve performance, this is no guarantee of use.

The evidence is from a laboratory experiment in which subjects were exposed to decision situations related to production planning, with variation in the level of aggregation in the information received.[9] Subjects using summary information achieved better results than those using raw data; however, it took them longer to reach their decisions and they had less confidence in them. Because the system that produced summary information led to better decisions, it was, by rational criteria, a "better" system than that which produced raw data. But because the "better" system demanded more decision time and left subjects with less confidence in their decisions, it is not at all clear that users would necessarily be motivated to use it. This assumption is borne out by a study of the use of computers by top management in Canada.[10] Lack of use of computers for important decisions was attributed in that study to lack of motivation; as its authors noted, "there is much desire but little passion." Thus the experiment quoted, together with frequent observations in the field of systems in disuse, must lead to the conclusion that a system which improves decisions will not necessarily generate use.

Users may be motivated to use a system by direct incentives external to the information system itself, however, as another laboratory experiment demonstrated. Half the subjects received monetary rewards tied to their profit performance, decision time, and other performance measures.[11] Paid subjects realized significantly greater profits while using more decision time than unpaid subjects. In both laboratory experiments, better decisions were related to longer decision times; the better users were those who were motivated by monetary rewards to devote more effort to their decisions even though the information system and its intrinsic rewards were identical.

Motivation to use a system apparently may be increased by a rewards system that is external to the MIS and independent of its attributes. Rewards could take the form of profit incentives, as in the experiment, bonuses for system use, public approbation by superiors, inclusion in promotion decisions, or any other form appropriate to the particular organization. Whatever form the incentives take, it seems clear that at the present stage of MIS development, direct rewards may be necessary to motivate use over and above the incentives provided intrinsically by the systems themselves.

Other User Characteristics

Some additional factors, either less important or less thoroughly studied, that affect use will be summarized in this section. Several factors will be dealt with under the heading of general managerial competence. The remaining factor is the age of users.

140

General Managerial Competence

A number of characteristics usually associated with managerial ability also appear to be associated with information system use. In other words, good managers also tend to be good users of information systems. The first characteristic of this type has nothing to do with MIS, systems, or computers; good users have to have a good level of general expertise in the functional area. Thus a manager who knows his business will also be a good MIS user.

Second, the ability to study new management methods and technologies contributes to information system use. Clearly, good managers in general should have this attribute.

A factor contributing frequently to MIS failure is the assumption commonly made by designers that managers need not understand how MIS work, only how to use them. True, it is not necessary that users become systems experts or as technically proficient as operators, but a basic knowledge and understanding of MIS is essential. Managers should be acquainted with the capabilities of computer systems and the current state of the art of MIS. They should also be aware of the major sources of data and of the alternative methods of data collection and information display.

Both factors indicate the necessity of managers being open to innovations and being capable of studying and absorbing them as they are introduced. Ongoing education and a willingness to devote time and effort to educational activities are necessary. The issue of education is discussed at length in the following section.

Age

Taylor studied the effect of age on managerial decision making and found that age is associated with a tendency to seek more information; older decision makers tend to take longer to reach decisions and have some difficulty in integrating information into accurate decisions, but they are able to diagnose the value of information more accurately than younger decision makers.[12] Taylor also found that older decision makers are less confident of their decisions and more flexible in changing their opinions when confronted with such new information as feedback on the consequences of their decisions. Although the effects of age on MIS use have not been studied directly, Taylor's study would seem to indicate that age is not an impediment to MIS use and may even lead to good use. Certainly the characteristics of older managers are those of good users.

User Attitudes Toward MIS

Positive user attitudes significantly enhance the likelihood of MIS success whereas hostile attitudes can contribute strongly to failure. The process by which these attitudes are determined is long and rather complicated, paralleling quite closely the process of MIS development; thus attitude formation should be considered an integral part of the development project and planned together with its other facets.

The relationship between users and implementors of MIS is an important factor in the establishment of user attitudes. This problem-prone relationship is fully discussed in chapter 8, which describes the relationships between the various groups of MIS actors. Because the user-implementor relationship is pertinent to an understanding of the process by which user attitudes are established, we will also briefly discuss it here.

The process of attitude formation is illustrated in figure 7-2. Potential users enter the process with prior attitudes toward MIS; these undergo change as a result of the users' experiences or involvement in the development and use of a system. Thus, posterior attitudes are derived from the effects of experience on prior attitudes. These effects are modulated by several factors that can contribute to the quality of the experience.

Prior Attitudes

One of the environmental variables affecting MIS success discussed in chapter 2 is the psychological climate in the organization. Attitudes were one factor mentioned as determining the psychological climate. That reference was to attitudes in the organization as a whole, not necessarily users' attitudes; but because users are managers in the organization accord-

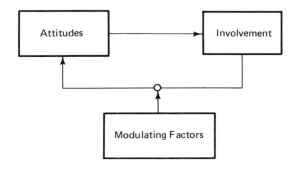

Figure 7-2. Attitudes, Involvement, and Modulating Factors

ing to our definition, it is clear that, as a group, their attitudes have an over-whelming effect on general organizational attitudes.

The attitude of the individual user is determined by two factors: the organizational environment and the individual's background. (The organizational attitude is the resultant of the vector of all individual attitudes and, in turn, each individual's attitude is affected by the attitudes of the community. This exemplifies why the behavioral variables are so dynamic, involved, and difficult to pin down for any but the briefest time.)

Guthrie studied the effects on the attitudes of users of years of service in the same organization, the functional area of the manager's job, and recent management training.[13] He found significant but moderate relationships between these personal characteristics and the individual's attitudes. In parallel, Guthrie measured indicators of the organizational and MIS environments, such as the rate of change of the information system and its sophistication. He concluded that the organizational and MIS environments rather than the backgrounds of individual managers were the key factor in attitude formation.

However, Lucas found no consistent relationship between situational factors and use.[14] Significantly, both studies strongly indicate that the *quality* of MIS affects users' attitudes. Rather than attempting to single out one factor that determines users' attitudes, we tend to view both as important for encouraging positive attitudes.

Prior attitudes towards MIS are molded by both the felt need for such systems and anticipations of their effects. Surveys of both top and middle management indicate that the felt need for MIS development is rather low, either because managers are satisfied with the systems they have or because they do not believe that formal systems can help them with their unstructured tasks, or perhaps their appreciation of such systems is too low.

The evidence on anticipated effects of MIS is not at all conclusive. One study found no support for the idea that managers are apprehensive about MIS.[15] Another, however, found a pervasive concern among managers for the effects of MIS on the people in the organization, attaining in some cases the proportions of a fear among managers of a loss of direct personal contact with fellow managers and employees.[16] Middle management's fears of being replaced by a computer may create an atmosphere conducive to rumors or false information that foster negative attitudes and resistance to change and innovation.

Because prior attitudes exist when the organization begins considering an MIS, it is not very reasonable to discuss ways of influencing them except in one sense: if management feels that it may embark on an MIS program at some future time, it could take steps to encourage favorable attitudes before it actually begins considering the system itself. This step would increase the perceived need for MIS and lessen apprehension about them to prepare the ground for actual execution. The following sections discuss the elements responsible for modification and change in prior attitudes in the process of implementing and operating MIS; some of these elements might be activated by management in anticipation of the initiation of any specific project to encourage favorable prior attitudes.

User Involvement

Involvement of potential users in the design, implementation, and operation of an MIS contributes to success. First, experienced operating managers are likely to be more fertile sources of ideas for profitable changes in operations than computer professionals. (Chapters 3 and 4 further elaborate the roles of users in MIS planning and implementation.)

The second mechanism through which user involvement affects MIS success is by positively influencing the prior attitudes of the users. Involvement of the users in the design of an MIS contributes to their feelings that they participated in its creation, that it is geared to their problems and meets their needs, and that they understand it. Involvement as users further increases understanding of the system and reduces fear of it. These two kinds of involvement have been termed "prior involvement" and "inquiry involvement."[17] Both kinds of involvement modify users' attitudes.

However, modifying effects are not necessarily positive; the direction of the change in attitudes also depends on the user's experience. Involvement with hardware-oriented, inflexible, and insensitive systems will foster negative attitudinal changes. Thus, on one hand, user involvement is essential for positive changes in attitudes, but on the other, the results may be negative if the experience is an unpleasant one. Thus involvement is essential, and care must be taken to ensure that its effects are desirable.

For user involvement to have favorable results, users should be involved intensively from the earliest stages of the project, certainly well before actual use takes place. Areas in which involvement is considered desirable include project selection, establishing system goals, project specifications, project planning, project staffing, responsibility for implementation progress and results, and establishing operating criteria. Participation by users is especially important in the project selection, planning, and implementation stages. Lack of involvement in these stages has been found by field surveys to contribute to system failure.

A major problem with attaining user involvement is the amount of time required. A survey of 2,000 middle managers in Canada found that although managers may want to have a lot of influence on the design and implementation of MIS, they are unwilling to devote the time, effort, and study required to make their participation meaningful.[18] The consequence is a widespread tendency for users to abdicate their responsibilities in system design to the computer specialists. Such lack of involvement, coupled with a natural tendency to change resistance (discussed in the next section), may result in a negative change in the prior attitudes of users.

Modulating Factors

Three factors that significantly influence the user's experience with involvement in MIS are education, the level of resistance to change, and the quality of the relationship between users and implementors.

User Education. Users must be educated to adopt positive attitudes if they are to attain maximum advantage from their use of MIS. Interestingly, recent training of *any* kind in management (not in information systems specifically) very clearly induces perceptions of need for, and positive effects of, information system change.

A quiet revolution in managers' attitudes toward MIS will probably occur in the foreseeable future as a result of the already widespread inclusion of computer, data-processing, and management information systems courses in college curricula generally and in business schools particularly. As the new generation of manager-users receives the relevant basic education, they will acquire positive attitudes toward MIS (which is also a major goal of this book). However, many managers already in responsible positions in industry have not had the benefit of such programs and special programs of education are required to acquaint them with this new technology. Heany warns that technical manuals, newsletters, pep talks, and goodwill cannot replace a well-designed, special-purpose educational program.[19] He views this task of educating users as part of the task of the MIS manager and recommends hiring professionals in management education.

Education is generally accepted as contributing to MIS success and to positively changing attitudes toward them. Argyris, however, questions whether such learning is transferable to conflict-provoking real-world situations.[20] He notes that MIS people, who presumably possess the requisite technical qualifications, have the same emotional problems dealing with each other as they have with line managers. This finding suggests that education must to a large extent be directed toward reducing change resistance and lowering the level of conflict between users and implementors, or else the fruits of education may be abandoned in the heat of interpersonal conflicts. Argyris suggests raising the interpersonal competence of both managers and MIS personnel in dealing with emotionality and strain. As interpersonal skills are improved, he believes that people will naturally turn to education.

Training has been widely used in conjunction with computer system introduction and many case studies have attributed MIS success, in part, to appropriate preparation of users for system introduction. However, user education cannot be successful as a one-time effort. After system implementation, an educational program must accompany actual use. Unpredicted problems, new methods of use, system shortcomings, changes in systems, possibilities for modification, new technologies, and new applications should all be part of the ongoing user education program.

Change Resistance. Nearly all MIS development studies indicate that it is a stressful process for participants that incurs heavy emotional and psychological costs at all levels of management and in many different types of organizations. The problems include changes in success criteria, fear of job downgrading and reduction of freedom of action, break-up of work relationships, perceived threats to decision-making functions and prerogatives of exercising managerial judgment, decreased feelings of essentiality, perceived threats to self-esteem, and psychological failure. These perceived effects can complicate the design process when they generate resistance. Resistance can range from apathy and quitting through open opposition and quiet destructiveness.

Totally negative views of the imposed changes tend to create genuine, though not necessarily malicious, resistance. The results are unresponsive and uncreative work behavior, uncertainty, anxiety, and even a surprising amount of sabotage. Because the introduction of computer systems can cause significant negative attitudinal changes that may adversely affect performance, successful MIS implementation depends on overcoming change resistance or at least containing it within reasonable bounds. Involving users in the development process may require that some initial resistance be overcome, but such positive experiences may break down resistance completely. An additional aid in reducing change resistance and improving user's attitudes is user education.

User-Implementor Relationships. One of the most important factors affecting MIS users' attitudes is their encounter with the MIS implementors. A good relationship may overcome unfavorable prior attitudes and change resistance, encourage user involvement, and promote user education. On the other hand, a conflict-prone relationship will probably aggravate unfavorable preconceptions, generate resistance, and generally alienate users from information systems and anything connected with them.

Even if user involvement in MIS design, implementation, and operation is initiated and sponsored by top management, the day-to-day contacts of the users will be with the implementors who are responsible for executing the program. Thus the best intentions of management may be foiled if the user-implementor relationship is unsatisfactory. Change resistance will be exacerbated or deadened, depending on the relationships that develop between users and implementors. These relationships will be fully discussed in chapter 8.

The main points in this chapter and their implications for MIS management are summarized in table 7-1.

Table 7-1
Summary of MIS User Variables

Variables	Conclusions
User requirements	System analysts should obtain as much information as possible about the decision problem from users and then complement it with their own expertise to produce an optimal definition of requirements.
	The higher in the organization a manager is placed, the more difficult it is to predict information needs in advance and the more one must rely on flexible systems to adapt to changing needs.
User rank	At the top management level, MIS are most useful in problem identification, analysis, and evaluation; because of the lack of structure in decision making at this level, MIS are less useful in formulating and selecting alternatives.
	The use of MIS at the highest levels of organizations will increase as people with information system training advance to those positions and as the relevant technologies develop.
Cognitive styles of users	The four basic styles of human, problem-oriented information processing are (1) receptive-systematic, (2) receptive-intuitive, (3) preceptive-systematic, and (4) preceptive-intuitive.
	Potential users will use information systems which are compatible with their cognitive styles and will not use those which are incompatible.
Motivation	Managers are generally not highly motivated to use information systems, even if they would improve their performance.
	Rewards geared to system use increase motivation.
Other user characteristics	The tendency to use MIS increases with general managerial competence and with age.
User attitudes	Prior attitudes toward MIS are composed of felt needs for such systems and of anticipation of their effects.
	Felt need is generally low and unfavorable effects are often anticipated.
	Management can positively influence attitudes by encouraging user involvement in project development.

Table 7-1 (cont.)

User training in information systems and general education in management increase involvement and foster positive attitudes.

The changes imposed by MIS development are often perceived as threatening to users and generate resistance to such changes. Positive involvement and experience tend to reduce change resistance.

Users' attitudes are heavily influenced by their relationships with system implementors. Enhancing interpersonal skills of users and implementors will tend to reduce the level of conflict between them and will encourage more positive attitudes.

Notes

1. Russel L. Ackoff, "Management Misinformation Systems," *Management Science*, vol. 14, no. 4 (December 1967), pp. 147-156.

2. J.C. Miller, "Conceptual Models for Determining Information Requirements," *Proceedings: Spring Joint Computer Conference, 1964* (Montvale, N.J.: AFIPS), pp. 609-620.

3. Arnoldo C. Hax, "Planning a Management Information System for a Distributing and Manufacturing Company," *Sloan Management Review*, vol. 14, no. 3 (Spring 1973), pp. 85-98.

4. William M. Zani, "Blueprint for MIS," *Harvard Business Review*, vol. 48, no. 6 (November-December 1970), pp. 95-100.

5. R.A. Kronenberg, "Weyerhaeuser's Management Information System," *Datamation*, vol. 13, no. 5 (May 1967), pp. 28-30.

6. Walter M. Carlson, "A Management Information System Designed by Managers," *Datamation*, vol. 13, no. 5 (May 1967), pp. 37-43.

7. Rodney H. Brady, "Computers in Top-Level Decision Making," *Harvard Business Review,* vol. 45, no. 4 (July-August 1967), pp. 67-76.

8. James L. McKenney and Peter G.W. Keen, "How Managers' Minds Work," *Harvard Business Review,* vol. 52, no. 3 (May-June 1974), pp. 79-90.

9. Norman L. Chervany and Gary W. Dickson, "An Experimental Evaluation of Information Overload in a Production Environment," *Management Science,* vol. 20, no. 10 (June 1974), pp. 1335-44.

10. Andrew A. Grindlay and Gordon Cummer, "Comment: Computer-Based Decision Systems and Canadian Mangement," *Management Science,* vol. 20, no. 4, Part II (December 1973), pp. 572-574.

11. Theodore F. Mock, "A Longitudinal Study of Some Information Structure Alternatives," *Data Base,* vol. 5, nos. 2, 3, and 4 (Winter 1973), pp. 40-49.

12. Ronald N. Taylor, "Age and Experience as Determinants of Management Information Processing and Decision Making Performance," *Academy of Management Journal,* vol. 18, no. 1 (March 1975), pp. 74-81.

13. Art Guthrie, "Attitudes of the User-Manager Towards Management Information Systems," *Management Informatics,* vol. 3, no. 5 (1974), pp. 221-232.

14. Henry C. Lucas, Jr., "Performance and the Use of an Information System," *Management Science,* vol. 21, no. 8 (April 1975), pp. 908-919.

15. Guthrie, "Attitudes of the User-Manager Towards Management Information Systems."

16. Grindlay and Cummer, "Comment: Computer-Based Decision Systems and Canadian Management."

17. E. Burton Swanson, "Management Information Systems: Appreciation and Involvement," *Management Science,* vol. 21, no. 2 (October 1974), pp. 178-188.

18. Guthrie, "Attitudes of the User-Manager Towards Management Information Systems."

19. Donald F. Heany, "Education: the Critical Link in Getting Managers To Use Management Systems," *Interfaces,* vol. 2, no. 3 (May 1972), pp. 1-7.

20. Chris Argyris, "Management Information Systems: The Challenge to Rationality and Emotionality," *Management Science,* vol. 17, no. 6 (February 1971), pp. B—275-B—291.

Suggested Readings

Ackoff, Russel L. "Management Misinformation Systems." *Management Science,* vol. 14, no. 4 (December 1967), pp. 147-156.

Brady, Rodney H. "Computers in Top-Level Decision Making." *Harvard Business Review,* vol. 45, no. 4 (July-August 1967), pp. 67-76.

Carlson, Walter M. "A Management Information System Designed by Managers." *Datamation,* vol. 13, no. 5 (May 1967), pp. 37-43.

Chervany, Norman L. and Dickson, Gary W. "An Experimental Evaluation of Information Overload in a Production Environment." *Management Science,* vol. 20, no. 10 (June 1974), pp. 1335-44.

Guthrie, Art. "Attitudes of the User-Manager Towards Management Information Systems." *Management Informatics,* vol. 3, no. 5 (1974), pp. 221-232.

McKenney, James L. and Keen, Peter G.W. "How Managers' Minds Work." *Harvard Business Review,* vol. 52, no. 3 (May-June 1974), pp. 79-90.

Swanson, E. Burton. "Management Information Systems: Appreciation and Involvement." *Management Science,* vol. 21, no. 2 (October 1974), pp. 178-188.

8

Intergroup Relationships

The last three chapters introduced and discussed the main groups of participants in MIS in terms of their skills and capabilities, MIS-related tasks, and rank in the organization. So far, however, each group has been considered separately; although hinted at, a discussion of the relationships between them was deferred to this chapter.

These three groups—top executives, users, and implementors—are functional, not personal, categories, because one person may appear in several of them. A top manager may be a user (although this is not yet very common), potential users may be assigned to implementation teams, and a top implementor may also be a top executive in the organization. (As we indicated in chapter 5, the direct use of MIS by top management for decision making is still rather rare; its use is virtually restricted to middle management. As a result, we do not attempt to distinguish between line management and users and in fact employ the terms interchangeably.) In the rather extended process of planning, design, implementation, and consequent use of an MIS, the three groups of participants are in constant interaction, with the resultant and ever-present possibility of friction and organizational stress. Thus, the organizational interrelationships inherent in MIS are an important feature of the implementation process that often cause complications and can influence system design.

The links between pairs of groups are discussed in this chapter, where relevant, in terms of communications, cooperation or conflict, and control relationships. A section is devoted to each pair—top management-user relations, top management-implementor relations, and user-implementor relations. For completeness, a fourth group is introduced that plays a part only after implementation; these are computer-dependent workers, whose relationships with the other groups are analyzed.

Top Management-User Relations

Communications: Encouragement to Participate

In chapter 7 we pointed out the importance of motivation to use MIS. Motivating users is one of the tasks of top management; its attitude is critical in promoting the participation of operating management in the information system effort. Top management can encourage use of MIS indirectly by creating an atmosphere favorable to an inquiring approach to problem solving, which is characterized by analysis of alternatives and model-based experimentation that lead naturally to the use of MIS. Further indirect encouragement may be provided by smoothing out differences between users and implementors and thereby fostering effective relationships between them.

Indirect encouragement, however, is not enough. Top management should go beyond stage-setting and should make the corporate commitment to MIS clear to operating executives. For example, Garrity cites an operating manager who made it clear that he did not volunteer to experiment with the computer, but it was spelled out to him by his superiors that he was to use the computer and "show results," so he did.[1] One of us witnessed the general manager of a division of a large aircraft corporation; he bluntly opened a panel discussion (at the end of a seminar on MIS for managers in his division) by making it clear that the division was committed to the MIS route and that the discussion should focus on the best way to go about it because the question of *whether* to develop MIS was no longer open to debate.

Communications: Asymmetry of Relations

The last anecdote could also be used to point out the main problem—the asymmetry of top management-user relations. Line managers do not generally have the experience, training, or power to challenge the decisions of higher levels of management. When top management is not open to line management suggestions, the resulting MIS may embody many of the dysfunctional aspects of existing systems while missing opportunities to realize potential benefits of the new technology. The authority of top management should express the organizational commitment to MIS and encourage the development of effective systems, not dictate specific details.

When a system is intended for use by both top and operating managements, however, some of the details pertinent to the efficacy of the system for the senior executives may clash with the needs of their juniors. In such cases, implementors will naturally tend to meet the needs of top management before those of operating management. This additional asymmetry is exemplified by time frames. The time span of top management decisions is longer than that for line management and MIS built to answer top management needs may be useless for middle management. Thus designing a system for use by several levels of management requires that the needs of each level be considered and the inconsistencies reconciled, otherwise the system will not be equally serviceable for all its designated clients.

151

Only if top management users keep lines of communication open for lower level users can the asymmetries in their relationships be overcome.

Top Mangement-Implementor Relations

Control

In chapter 4, we discussed the stages of the MIS project. A critical aspect of development is the smooth alternation of execution and control phases. This section deals with the same topic in terms of those responsible for the phases rather than of the phases themselves. Clearly, implementors are responsible for the execution cycles and top management for the control cycles. In this relationship top management, in the control phases, evaluates the performance of implementors in the execution phases.

Skilled professionals look for approbation from their professional peers and colleagues rather than from the organizations in which they happen to work. Although top management is usually competent in such functional areas as production, marketing and finance, only a few top executives are acquainted with the MIS function because it is a new profession. As a result, top executives encounter difficulties in attempting to control the information system function and its computer professional executives.

Several symptoms of such difficulties faced by top management have already been indicated. In chapter 6 we noted that the selection process for MIS executives is particularly ineffective because of the newness of the profession and the inward orientation of its practitioners. Top management also faces great difficulties in extracting performance commitments from the MIS chief. Though top executives view control as a natural part of their job, implementors complain that they are unable to perform creatively with management breathing down their necks. It is not surprising, therefore, that few organizations have developed effective control procedures for MIS. However, if MIS are to be developed on time and within budget and to perform effectively, top management must institute formal planning, reporting, and evaluation procedures.

Communications

Good communications between top management and implementors are essential for two reasons. First, the MIS director needs easy access to top management to obtain the organizational commitments and resources he needs to function effectively. Such access also provides the backing the MIS needs to weather inevitable conflicts with users, who will usually call on pressing operational considerations to support their own view. Second, only good communications will enable top management to imbue MIS executives with an understanding of organizational goals for information systems. In one case it took more than a year to convince the computer organization that the criteria for evaluating the system were based on efficient use of management time rather than on efficient use of machine time.[2] Close communications reduce such misunderstandings.

Organizations sometimes attempt to facilitate communications between management and implementors by placing the MIS function close to top management. Argyris reports a case in which the MIS team was housed in a management services division, supposed to ease access to top management.[3] In practice, however, access was not easy. Thus a favorable location is not sufficient, but management must also be prepared to expend the time and effort required for establishing open channels with MIS leadership. (For an extended discussion of this problem, see chapter 5.)

User-Implementor Relations

Communications

Not only are good communications necessary between implementors and top management, but they are also essential between implementors and users. In fact, however, rampant communications problems between implementors and users often inhibit MIS success. A major cause of these communication problems is the unbridged culture gap between the two groups. Computer technicians form a separate subculture that has its own extensive and incomprehensible vocabulary and jargon, a subculture which delights in technical sophistication and tends to prefer complex to simple solutions. (Robert Townsend, former chairman of the board of Avis, has described this subculture: "most of the computer technicians that you're likely to meet or hire are complicators, not simplifiers. They're trying to make it look tough. Not easy. They're building a mystique, a priesthood, their own mumbo-jumbo ritual to keep you from knowing what they—and you—are doing."[4])

The uninitiated user coming into contact with this subculture tends to be either intimidated or angered when confronted by technological arguments that he cannot follow and that prove why the things he wants cannot be done and why those he does not want must be done.

The communications problems arising from the existence of the computer subculture are often exacerbated by frequent differences in cognitive styles between implementors and users. In the cognitive dimensions introduced in chapter 7, information systems people tend generally to be receptive and systematic. Users will often be preceptive and intuitive—the opposite of the implementor type. Such differences in cognitive styles tend to aggravate the communications problem.

The solution to the communications problem probably lies mainly with the users, because implementors are largely its cause and have little motivation for solving it. First, users can learn the technology sufficiently to understand and evaluate the implementors' arguments. Second, users must not accept the implementors' arguments or agree to their solutions until they are fully understood. If users insist on complete explanations before agreeing to solutions, implementors will find it expedient to phrase their arguments more intelligibly and, in time, the communications problem will be alleviated.

Conflict

A communications problem occurs when both sides are willing to cooperate but find it difficult because they lack common assumptions and a common language. Such problems are often fertile ground for the generation of conflict, which occurs when the parties are no longer interested in cooperation and are in covert or even open opposition.

Conflict between users and implementors is expressed in unfavorable attitudes, unwillingness to cooperate, and users' refusal to participate in design and operation of the system. In its extreme forms, conflict may lead to quitting, apathy, open opposition, and even sabotage. Conflict may lead the implementors to ignore the advice of line managers and to reject ideas generated by them, no matter how good or relevant. In such an atmosphere of unresponsive and uncreative work behavior, no MIS can succeed.

Two major reasons seem to cause conflict between users and implementors—change resistance and power relocation. Of course, change resistance is by no means specific to MIS and has to be overcome whenever changes are implemented. People know the existing situation, adapt themselves to it, function in it, and often feel comfortable with it. Change implies unknowns and uncertainties that frighten people and lead them to resist it, especially when change is imposed and not chosen. The introduction of an MIS is a change at the top of the organization that affects managers, especially the middle echelon of management, whose power to resist change is considerably greater than that of lower level employees. Change as such, however, is probably not the main reason for conflict between implementors and managers-users; rather it is the particular kind of change that relocates power in the organization and diminishes the power of users.

In chapter 1 we showed that management information systems collect information from different functional areas, integrate and process it, and then distribute it to those who need it. In such an organizational design,

competence and cooperation become ascendent over the traditional depart-
mentalized organization in which the departments are in competition and
each seeks to maximize its power. Unfortunately, the MIS development
process itself accentuates the shift in power that accompanies it. Whisler
suggests that during the development of new systems, top management en-
trusts middle management with decisions in their areas of expertise, providing them with a highly active and powerful role during the transition to
the new system, especially if they choose to become actively involved.[5]
When the transition is completed, some of middle management's responsibilities have been incorporated into programmed decision rules and many
middle management people have reduced responsibilities for direct decision
making. A specialization effect also occurs as the more creative aspects of
decision making tend to move from line to staff people. Those with line
responsibility may lose, or feel they have lost, the authority to deal with ex-
ceptions and problems of change. As a gradual transfer of power takes
place to the information services group, users become less powerful and
more frustrated, and the frustration finds its outlet in open conflict.

Middle managers at the staff level who fear being displaced by a computer often view the MIS executive with suspicion or hostility. A comparison of the opposition of managers to the managerial revolution sparked
by the computer with the opposition of laborers to machines at the beginning of the Industrial Revolution is inescapable. We hope that the general
effects of this revolution, sometimes called the "second industrial revolution," will be as beneficial as those of the first.

Conflict Reduction

A case has been made that conflict between users and MIS executives is
nearly unavoidable because of the catch under which the information chief
operates; if he goes slowly, he will be accused of allowing stagnation in the
name of stability, but if he goes quickly, he will be accused of introducing
change for the sake of progress or keeping up with the state of the art.[6]
Whatever he does will be criticized on the assumption that he has his own
ulterior motives. If this occurs and conflict is inevitable or very prevalent,
efforts should be made to minimize it.

Education of both implementors and users is widely recommended as a
means of conflict reduction. If the educational program is successful, users
will know more about MIS and implementors will better understand and be
more sensitive to users' problems. Education therefore improves communications.

Improving communications can assist in containing conflict. A good
understanding of the system will, at least, ensure that the conflict is over the
real issues of change and is not compounded by false rumors and groundless

fears. Because conflict is the result of the organizational changes accompanying MIS and because improving communications does not eliminate the changes, solving the communications problem will not resolve the conflict but can prevent it from becoming irrational.

Several other steps help to reduce friction between users and implementors, including role definition, formalization of procedures, and heightening implementors' sensitivity to users.

Role Definition. Inconsistencies in the perceptions of implementors and users each about the other's roles in relation to MIS cause much conflict. Users may assume that implementors serve their current needs, while implementors may assume that their task is to improve the decision-making practices of users. To avoid this source of conflict, roles should be clearly defined. The terms of reference of each group should state clearly what their task is and where their responsibilities begin and end.

A related issue is status. If users and implementors are of greatly different status in the organization, the group with the higher status will naturally feel competent to impose its views on the other party. Such incongruence allows unclear role definitions and unwillingness to accept whatever definitions may exist. Thus gross inconsistencies in status should be avoided. This issue has already been dealt with from a slightly different angle under the heading of "rank" in the previous chapters. Clearly, however, status involves more than the formal rank of each group but includes such factors as the time and interest devoted to it by top management and the resources at its disposal.

Formalization. Without clear project management guidelines, implementors and users must develop their own procedures for dealing with each other. Clearly, this process can breed conflict. Thus the administrative and organizational processes between the two groups should be carefully formalized to facilitate unambiguous communication. The performance standards, short-term control, and feedback devices should be formalized for the more routine aspects of project development. Formal procedures should also be designed to remove MIS personnel from frequent *informal* interaction with users; it is in informal discussions and conclusions, in which each side understands what it wants to understand, that the seeds of conflict are often sown.

Sensitivity to Users. Users of MIS, who are line managers, are entrusted with the daily operations of the organization. For them, involvement in system development is an additional burden, often undesired and frequently resented. Developing MIS, however, is the implementor's main job. Thus the onus for obtaining the cooperation of users falls largely on the MIS staff. Successfully discharging this duty depends heavily on implementors' sensitivity to the needs and attitudes of users.

Sensitivity to users' needs is reflected in the way the implementors design their systems. Systems should be attuned to the informational needs of the users, using in-depth informational analysis as a basis. Information analysis is not only a basis for defining system requirements, but it is also a formal means for establishing and facilitating communications between implementors and users. Thus information analysis is a highly regarded and much advocated tool of the MIS implementor.

Sensitivity to users' attitudes is the basis for successful tactics of implementation. Because users generally resent the change and loss of power associated with the introduction of MIS, implementors should strive to minimize users' perceptions of these effects. If systems are changed frequently, especially without asking the users, both the rate of change to which they must adjust increases and their loss of discretion is emphasized. Clearly, frequent changes to systems should be avoided; when unavoidable, they should be coordinated with users.

In the same vein, implementation practices should take into account the relative importance of the different managers using various types of information, which includes recognizing that the importance of the information derives from the importance of the manager using it. Deviation from this rule again underscores managers' loss of power and must generate opposition. Systems must also be built to accommodate the cognitive styles of MIS users, which are generally more intuitive and less analytical than those of implementors. Only a high degree of sensitivity to users will enable implementors to see their counterparts' point of view; successful system personnel do, however, learn that they must take managers' attitudes and preferences into account.

Cooperation

Of course, the goal is to achieve active cooperation between implementors and users, not merely to avoid conflict. The sharp distinctions between MIS people and line managers will probably tend to diminish in the future as information systems courses become generally incorporated in management curricula and as, with the spread of MIS, managers come into contact with them from the beginning of their careers.[7] Until information systems become an area that every manager is expected to understand, efforts are necessary to achieve cooperation between the two as yet distinct functions.

Cooperation between the two groups is especially critical because neither the manager nor the analyst alone can design and implement an MIS. Attempts have been made in both directions—corporate models designed by experts and imposed on the organization and the inside-out approach, by which, theoretically, managers can do without implementors. In practice, however, successful systems are always joint ventures; cooperative teamwork and dialogue are essential.

Argyris reports a case in which the solution chosen was to place members of line management on MIS teams to act as a liaison; these managers reported great role strain, being torn between loyalty to their peers in management and their desire to see the system succeed, but made significant inputs to the development of the system.[8] If friction between the two groups can be avoided and active involvement of managers achieved, then the probability for success is considerably enhanced.

Computer-Dependent Workers

Our discussion of relationships within the context of MIS would be incomplete without mentioning computer-dependent workers, those employees who are associated with the information system as recorders of input data or receivers of the output, but not for decision-making purposes. They are almost invariably clerical personnel, but in certain cases managers may also perform these functions. These people interact with all the other groups, especially implementors and users. It is unnecessary, however, to distinguish between the specific relationships.

Studies of the resistance to change initiated by MIS development among such workers show that in its overt aggressive forms it can be expressed in violent outspokenness and deliberately erroneous data entry.[9] In its less aggressive forms resistance consists of spreading unfavorable rumors and carelessness, but not wantonly erroneous data input. The remedies we recommend are the same as those recommended for overcoming change resistance in general—participation in design of input documents and work methods, education, and open channels of communication.

It is most important that these employees have a clear picture of what is going to happen with the introduction of the new system. The positive features of the new system, from their point of view, should be emphasized and the negative features openly communicated. Special care should be taken to clarify the personnel policy that will accompany the new system; how will new employees be recruited, what will happen to veteran employees remaining in the system, and what awaits those who become redundant? Frank answers to such questions will at least minimize the amount of unbased rumormongering and, if the policy has been well thought out, may alleviate most of the fears that generate resistance.

Because computer-dependent workers frequently do not see the end product of their work, they feel little responsibility for it and may become unreliable. Feedback to such workers indicating that their data are actually used as well as control of and feedback on error rates together with bonuses for accurate work may greatly alleviate this problem. Inaccuracies are also sometimes the result of faulty communications. System designers tend to write instructions in their own jargon and geared to their own level that are often unclear or simply incomprehensible to the employees for whom they are intended. Operating procedures should be clear to the personnel who are to be directed by them.

In summary, most of the resistance among computer-dependent workers arises from uncertainty and a fear of the unknown. The way to minimize this resistance is through good communications. The clearer it is to these employees during the implementation process what awaits them at the end of it and the better they understand their role in the system when it becomes operational, the less serious their fears will be, the lower their level of resistance, and the greater their feeling of participation in the system.

The main points covered in this chapter on interrelationships between the groups of personnel connected with MIS are summarized in table 8-1.

Table 8-1
Summary of Intergroup Relationship Variables

Variables	Conclusions
Top management-user relations	Top management should encourage users, directly and indirectly, to participate in all stages of the MIS effort and should make clear the organizational commitment to MIS.
	Top management should keep lines of communication open to users and should be receptive to their suggestions in regard to MIS.
Top management-implementor relations	Formal controls and evaluation procedures should be established on implementors by top management.
	Good communications between top management and implementors provide support for the implementors and improve their understanding of organizational goals.
User-implementor relations	Communications problems between implementors and users are rampant and often inhibit the success of MIS. Users should refuse to approve recommendations until they understand them fully.
	Conflict between users and implementors is caused by change resistance and power relocation and is difficult to avoid.
	Conflict may be reduced by education, improving communications, role definition, formalization of user-implementor relationships, and increasing implementors' sensitivity to users' problems.

Table 8-1 (cont.)

	Neither the manager nor the analyst can design and implement an MIS; cooperation, teamwork, and dialogue are essential.
Computer-dependent workers	It is important that computer-dependent workers have a clear picture of how the MIS plan will affect them. Their contribution to the system should be explained and they should be provided with feedback on their performance.

Notes

1. John T. Garrity, "Top Management and Computer Profits," *Harvard Business Review,* vol. 41, no. 4 (July-August 1963), pp. 6-12, 172-174.

2. Walter M. Carlson, "A Management Information System Designed by Managers," *Datamation,* vol. 13, no. 5 (May 1967), pp. 37-43.

3. Chris Argyris, "Management Information Systems: The Challenge to Rationality and Emotionality," *Management Science,* vol. 17, no. 6, (February 1971), pp. B-275–B-291.

4. Robert Townsend, *Up the Organization* (New York: Knopf, 1970, p. 36).

5. Thomas Whisler, *The Impact of Computers on Organizations* (New York: Praeger, 1970).

6. Cyrus F. Gibson and Richard L. Nolan "Managing the Four Stages of EDP Growth," *Harvard Business Review,* vol. 52, no. 1 (January-February 1974), pp. 76-88.

7. See, for example, Robert G. Murdick and Joel E. Ross, "Future Management Information Systems," *Journal of Systems Management,* part I, vol. 23, no. 4 (April 1972), pp. 22-25; and part II, vol. 23, no. 5 (August 1972), pp. 32-35.

8. Argyris, "Management Information Systems: The Challenge to Rationality and Emotionality."

9. Donald L. Caruth, "Basic Psychology for a System Change," *Journal of Systems Management,* vol. 25, no. 2 (February 1974), pp. 10-13.

Suggested Readings

Argyris, Chris. "Management Information Systems: The Challenge to Rationality and Emotionality." *Management Science,* vol. 17, no. 6 (February 1971), pp. B-275–B-291.

Caruth, Donald L. "Basic Psychology for A System Change." *Journal of Systems Management,* vol. 25, no. 2 (February 1974), pp. 10-13.

McKinsey & Co. Inc. "Unlocking the Computer's Profit Potential: A Research Report to Management." *The McKinsey Quarterly* (Fall 1968).

Whisler, Thomas. *The Impact of Computers on Organizations.* New York: Praeger, 1970.

9

The Structure of MIS: A Summary and Conclusions

This book addresses the problem of constructing successful management information systems. We have discussed the process of constructing such systems (chapters 2 through 4) and the actors participating in the process (chapters 5 through 8). Throughout the process of development, decisions are made and actions taken that determine the structure of the system in which the process culminates. A given MIS structure is the end product of the development process. Thus, a survey of the characteristics that compose the structure of the system reorganizes much of the information we have discussed in a way that concentrates all the aspects of the process that affect a single structural variable in one section. At the end of this chapter, we also present some general conclusions relating to MIS and their development.

In their seminal paper "A Program for Research on Management Information Systems," Mason and Mitroff defined an information system as consisting "of at least one PERSON of a certain PSYCHOLOGICAL TYPE who faces a PROBLEM within some ORGANIZATIONAL CONTEXT for which he needs some EVIDENCE to arrive at a solution and that the evidence is made available to him through some MODE OF PRESENTATION."[1]

First, we discuss the information attributes of MIS; they constitute the structure of the system and are the dependent variables in system development. This structure corresponds to Mason and Mitroff's "EVIDENCE" and "MODE OF PRESENTATION." The degree to which this structure is likely to be successful depends on the extent to which it meshes with the independent variables—Mason and Mitroff's "PERSON of a certain PSYCHOLOGICAL TYPE," which we refer to as *individual fit* and their "ORGANIZATIONAL CONTEXT," which we have called *organizational fit*. The final element of Mason and Mitroff's definition, the "PROBLEM," or, in the management context, the decision situation, has been discussed in chapter 2 under the heading "Nature of the Problem."

Thus, structuring MIS is making decisions about the parameters of systems to fit them to a specific organization and the individual users in that organization as figure 9-1 illustrates. There are three dimensions—system characteristics, individual fit, and organizational fit. The structure of the MIS is given by the values of the system characteristics, detailed on the top of the three-dimensional figure. The values of the system characteristics should be set to achieve good fit with individual managers separately and

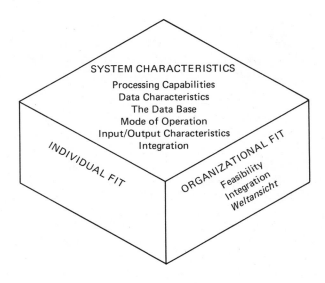

Figure 9-1. Dimensions of MIS Structure

with the organization as a whole. Although most aspects of individual and organizational fit have been discussed, they are scattered throughout the book. These aspects are collected and discussed as units in the second and third parts of this chapter, following the discussion of system characteristics.

System Characteristics

The structure of an MIS is the combination of the values of a rather long list of parameters that determine its technical character. The values of these parameters are implicit in the requirements definition of the MIS target and materialize during the implementation process. Thus the structure of a system is a realization of the system requirements, which can be classified into six groups: processing capabilities, data characteristics, the data base, the mode of operation, input-output characteristics, and integration. The boundaries between these groups are not very clear; the data base contains elements of processing capabilities, the input-output characteristics are closely related to the mode of operation, and so on. We will elaborate some of these relationships while examining the variables.

Processing Capabilities

The processing capabilities of a system are its facilities for filtering, aggregating, and manipulating data. They determine the system's ability to reduce data and use them analytically in decision rules, models, and simulations. There are many possibilities for manipulating data, but it is clear that decision makers should be provided with flexible tools for manipulating and analyzing relevant data; the data themselves should be directly accessible or, at least, readily available. This availability includes the ability of users to interact with all the data in the system, not just with some preselected subset.

The importance of advanced data processing capabilities arises from considerations related to the cognitive styles of users—an issue discussed at some length in chapter 7. Because different users have different cognitive styles, they require that information be presented to them after different types and levels of processing. One of the simplest processes, aggregation, has been studied relatively extensively.

One experiment on aggregation found that subjects who received more detailed feedback performed better than subjects with summary feedback information.[2] This finding seems to support contentions that because most users have grown up in environments with limited data-processing power, they are used to receiving detailed reports; therefore they do not know how to cope with summary information[3] and, also, there is a degree of aggregation beyond which the information becomes too general and thus useless for decision making.[4] A different experiment, however, found the opposite result—decision makers given simple summary data made higher quality decisions than those receiving the same data in detail, although they did take longer to make their decisions and had less confidence in them.[5]

How can we reconcile these apparently conflicting results? We suggest that there is an optimal level of aggregation for each decision maker in each decision problem; too little aggregation equals too much information, and the user will suffer from information overload—he will not be able to see the forest for the trees. Too much aggregation equals too little information, and the user will not have enough information to make a decision—he will be groping in the dark. To achieve an optimal amount of information, each user should be able to determine the level and type of aggregation he wants—whether subtotals and totals, averages, frequencies, distributions, fractiles, standard deviations, or variances. As an example, one of the goals of a system designed at Weyerhaeuser Corporation was to supply managers with "the right amount of information."[6]

Data Characteristics

The processing capabilities discussed in the previous section are required to permit the production of data with characteristics conducive to effective use. In this section we will survey the major attributes or characteristics of data, such as content, accuracy, recency, frequency, and feedback time.

Content. The content, or relevance, of data is determined by several decisions, the first of which relates to the boundaries of the data incorporated. This decision determines which items of data will be included in the system and which excluded. Thus, a decision that a system will maintain data on certain products for five years also implies that older data and data on other products will be excluded.

If the MIS is based on an analytical or simulation model, the design of the model prescribes the exact nature of the data. In this case, the decision on data content is part of the model design, in the course of which the availability of the data must be considered.

In the past, most systems concentrated on quantitative data. Several authorities, however, have stressed the importance of verbal and contextual information in managerial decision making.[7] In practice, systems containing verbal information are becoming more common especially in intelligence data bank applications.

The level of aggregation discussed in the preceding section is also related to data content. Storing data in disaggregated form permits any level of aggregation to be achieved, but raises storage and processing costs. Furthermore, disaggregated storage leads to an observed tendency to store large quantities of data that are never used. Thus the costs of disaggregation should be balanced against the need to provide managers with the desired degree of detail.

Accuracy. Accuracy is measured by the rate of errors in the data. Great importance is often attributed to this characteristic and efforts are made to eliminate or at least minimize errors, usually at considerable cost. It seems to us that much of this effort may be wasted. Exertions to minimize errors are based on the assumption that the managerial decision process is sensitive to small variations in the data. This may be true at the lowest levels; for example, our bank must exert itself to keep our account 100 percent accurate. But the higher one goes in the management hierarchy, clearly the less sensitive decisions are to small deviations in information inputs. If we are considering a $1 million loan to XYZ Corporation, does it really matter whether its current indebtedness is $8.85 million or $8.87 million?

This is not to say that any amount of error is tolerable, but given the nature of top-level decision making there is clearly a limit to the resources which should be expended on maximizing accuracy. Because a high level of accuracy also requires several correction cycles, it takes a long time to achieve and is at the expense of the next data characteristic—recency.

Recency. Recency, or information delay, relates to the degree to which the data are current. The evidence accumulated from surveys and experiments tends to indicate that the importance of timeliness in data is underestimated.[8] A major reason why managers bypass information systems is that they are unable to obtain the data they need within the time frame dictated by the decision situation. Thus data need to be continuously updated to be relevant whenever needed, even at very short notice. The usefulness of data decreases rapidly with age and, in many situations, rapid and recent information is more important than accurate information.

Frequency. The frequency parameter is relevant mainly for systems based on periodic report cycles. Frequency refers to the period elapsing between reports in such a system. In systems based on report cycles that have no facilities for queries between reports, the frequency of report cycles also determines the recency of the data available. There is a clear tendency, however, both in administrative and in management information systems to provide real-time query facilities. The more widespread such facilities become, the less the importance of this characteristic.

Feedback Time. Feedback time is closely related to the preceding characteristics; it is the time elapsing between the moment of decision and the availability of a report on the effect of the decision on the environment. Thus, feedback time is the sum of the times required for the decision to be implemented and for the data on the effects of the decision to be collected, input, processed, and output. The length of the data-processing stages of the feedback cycle, relative to the length of time of the decision implementation and of the decision cycle itself, determines how useful the information will be.

The range of values that these five characteristics can assume in a particular system determine the degree of flexibility of the system and the possibilities for adapting it to the needs and cognitive styles of the managers who use it. Clearly, the better the performance of the system on each of the dimensions discussed, the more sensitive the system will be to its clients' individual requirements.

The Data Base

Once data have been collected and stored, they are not necessarily available for ready manipulation and use. Data bases provide such capabilities in a reasonably efficient manner. A data base is a collection of logical data served by a data-base management system, which updates the data collection and retrieves extracts from it on request. This definition raises the question whether all aspects of MIS are subsumed under the heading of data bases. One authority has, in fact, gone so far as to state that the whole issue of MIS will reduce to data bases.[9]

The importance of a data base is exemplified by the following case report.[10] A large corporation was considering a new marketing strategy that would affect warehouse capacity requirements. Because the corporation already had an inventory simulation, sales forecasting programs, and a market penetration model, the chief executive assumed that he would be able to evaluate the effect of the proposed marketing strategy on the warehouses immediately. In fact, however, although all the necessary data was in storage, it was locked into the standard system; it would have taken a year to answer the president's question. The data-base approach is oriented to providing greater flexibility in data manipulation and to prevent this kind of impasse.

A data-base system provides the requisite flexibility, primarily by a sophisticated structuring of the data, which allows any combination of data items to be extracted as needed without prior planning. Conventional data files are structured to permit periodic preparation of preplanned, structured reports; in such systems, the preparation of unscheduled reports requires that the data be copied and the copy processed and restructured to provide the new report. This process is often so time-consuming that the special reports are obsolete by the time they are produced. The complex structuring of data in a data-base system greatly increases the *responsiveness* of such systems to managers' needs.

Data independence also increases the flexibility of data-base systems. In conventional systems, each application stores and updates its own data; these data are then not readily available to other applications or for joint processing with other data collections. When a data-base system is installed, data are sequestered from the individual applications and concentrated in the data base where all data are equally available to all applications, including new applications and special processing. This accessibility is especially important for decision models; because such models are often developed on an ad hoc basis for solving unique and nonrecurrent problems they do not have their own data collections. However, all the data in a data base are available to modelers and decision makers anywhere in the organization and whatever their relationship to the function that generates the data.

Under the conventional system in which each application maintains its own data, there is considerable redundancy because many data items will be required by more than one application. Because different applications have different update cycles, the same data item may appear with a different value in each report in which it appears, causing confusion and uncertainty. Furthermore, the same data item, or rather a data item with a given name, may have a different meaning in each application in which it appears.

(This problem was brought home very forcibly to one of us during a recent consulting job. The client was a large winery that was encountering customer dissatisfaction because it frequently accepted orders for items which it later found were out of stock and could not be delivered. We found that the firm had two definitions of inventory—one for tax purposes, which included all stock within the plant gate, and the other for its own use, which included all stock in the warehouse but excluded stock already packed and on the loading dock. The sales department used the latter information as the basis for confirming orders. The stock in the warehouse, however, included quantities that had already been earmarked for shipment but had not yet been packed. Thus the sales department could not obtain the figure it really needed—stock on hand and not yet committed. Clearly, a more rigorous definition of the various types of inventory was needed in this case.)

Concentrating data in a common data base eliminates redundancies. Because each data item appears once in the data base, it will have a standard meaning and value for all users. Thus the concentration of data in a common data base also increases *data integrity*.

The capabilities required of a data-base system follow from the preceding discussion of possible goals for such a system. The discussion of these capabilities is rather technical; however, a large selection of books deals with this topic in considerable detail.[11]

Data-Base Development. Once the decision has been made to undertake data-base development, two main questions need to be answered. First, which data should be stored in the data base and, second, should the data base be built up from existing files or from scratch?

The first question is really an appendix to the issue of data content. In the context of a data base, not only must the decision be made which data items to include in the data base, but these items must be uniquely defined and named to prevent redundancies and inconsistencies. When two different data items have the same name, a decision has to be made whether both are necessary, in which case they will require precise definition and at least one will have to be renamed. If it is concluded that one item is sufficient, one will have to be chosen. If the same item is entered into the system at more than one point, it will also be necessary to determine which source will continue to supply the item and who will be responsible for maintaining and updating it. Thus, in addition to determining data content, the data base design includes a rationalization of the data storage and processing functions.

There are varying answers to the second question—whether existing files should be incorporated in the data base or whether a fresh start is preferable. One approach suggests that the data base be developed gradually by first adding an ad hoc response capability to existing files to improve service to users, while deferring the integration of the files to opportune moments as they arise. Another approach, however, suggests that it is a mistake to attempt to build MIS on the basis of files designed for other purposes and that a reinitiation is preferable. In practice, both strategies may be observed. When existing files lend themselves to rapid response and provide good service, it is probably preferable to undertake a more evolutionary course of data-base development. However, when existing files contain bad inconsistencies or their structuring does not permit adequate responsiveness, there will probably be no alternative to completely restructuring the data base to eliminate redundancies or to improve response time or both.

Mode of Operation

There is a sharp dividing line between the two basic modes of operation—batch processing, in which data are batched and processed periodically to provide information on a deferred basis, and on-line real-time (OLRT), which processes data continuously and provides immediate response. The number of applications and size of systems devoted to real-time processing have steadily increased. In numerous business and non-business applications, on-line real-time capabilities are considered virtually mandatory—for example, industrial process control, military command systems, airline and hotel reservations, and retail banking.

Time-sharing leads to faster problem solving and higher quality solutions, which has been well documented in one MIS case.[12] At Xerox (Canada) time-shared models have proven successful in assisting in corporate planning. The OLRT mode of operation reduced information overload on managers and the payoffs of computer-based models were increased when functional management could execute them directly to assist in their decision processes. This type of direct interaction between managers and computerized decision aids is becoming increasingly common; in a survey several years ago, 350 of 600 respondents to a questionnaire replied that their organization had installed some kind of terminal device connected to an on-line system for use by management level people.[13]

The effect of the mode of operation on user behavior has probably been more thoroughly studied than all other system characteristics. These studies indicate a 20 percent man-hour advantage in favor of time-shared problem solving while 40 percent more computer time is used in time-sharing than in batch. Thus the user trades off computer time for his own time. When only computer time and man hours are taken into account, the costs are about balanced and neither system shows clear economic advantages. However, the fact that problem-solving performance is improved by time-sharing clearly makes it the preferable mode of operation. Given the constantly rising costs of manpower and declining costs of computers, the direct cost tradeoff will also tend to favor time-sharing.

The main behavioral result of on-line-off-line studies is the existence of very large differences in human performance, differences which are typically an order of magnitude larger than computer system differences. The importance of this factor is exemplified by an experiment.[14] In a scheduling decision problem, it was found that although participants possessed information-processing and decision-making capabilities to achieve better performances, they used them only in special circumstances. The imposition of a different decision rule produced considerably improved performance, despite the participants' genuinely held beliefs that no major change was possible. This experiment emphasizes that it is not sufficient to provide a technically efficient MIS, but users must also be motivated to use the system if it is to be effective.

Another significant behavioral aspect of time-shared problem solving is that users do most of their thinking and spend most of their time away from the computer terminal. Thus, man-computer problem solving consists mainly of introspection or man-to-man communication and major insights occur away from the terminal. Despite "man-machine symbiosis" and other such science-fictional notions, time-shared problem solving is still a human-directed process; the user is the central source of strategic intelligence and the computer is a tactical aid.

Input-Output Characteristics

The input-output element of MIS structure deals with the interface between the user and the system. Although it is a technical rather than a substantive issue, it has considerable impact on the attitudes of managers towards management information systems. Consequently, the input-output characteristics have considerable influence on the degree of use of MIS and, hence, on their success.

The unifying factor by which input-output characteristics may be evaluated is their degree of naturalness. The more natural the input or the output to the manager, the greater the likelihood that he will use the system. Inputs and outputs should be simple and expressed in familiar forms that are easily understood. Thus, standard English usage enhances MIS use, while extensive use of jargon, codes, and symbols drives managers away. Furthermore, the presentation of data in narrative form embedded in a story or character-laden context is more attractive than abstract impersonal information.[15]

In a somewhat more limited sense, the issue of context also applies to report formats. Bad formats are a frequent cause of low use of systems. They result from several factors: first, the lack of involvement, or lack of knowledge, on the part of managers who let implementors design information formats for them rather than specifying their needs themselves; and second, even when managers are involved in report specification, the long lead times in project development often cause the formats to obsolesce by the time they become operational. In general, report formats tend to be stagnant and difficult to change, while managers' needs are dynamic and ever-changing.

An additional aspect of input-output characteristics is the medium or mode of communication. To date it is almost universally written, whether in the form of printed reports or on display terminals. Some evidence, however, indicates that people perform better with verbal than with written inputs and that managers, specifically, favor verbal channels of communication.[16] Although still in their infancy, verbal input and output units are already available commercially; if, in fact, verbal communications improve performance and increase use, we may expect a considerable increase in the use of voice systems as they become more efficient and less expensive.

Integration

Throughout this book we have used the term MIS to indicate a collection, or federation, of management information systems with varying degrees of integration. Thus, the degree of integration is a measure of the extent to which any such collection of systems approaches the ultimate goal of a completely integrated system representing the total organization.

There are several aspects to integration in the context of MIS: integration of data, integration of models, integration of models with the data base, and integration in use. Integration of data is the systematization of data from different areas or levels in the organization. The current technological vehicle for such integration is, of course, the data-base system. The higher the degree of integration, the more functional areas and the more hierarchical levels contribute data to common data bases.

Integration of models refers to the degree to which outputs of models become inputs to other models—for example, when the results of a sales forecasting model become input to a production planning model or a plant cash flow projection becomes part of a divisional financial forecast.

The third dimension is the degree of integration of models with the data base—the degree to which the models draw their inputs from a common data base and put their outputs back into it. With a low degree of integration, each model will have to prepare its own data, with the consequent redundancies and inconsistencies discussed earlier. A high degree of integration of models with the data base also indicates a high degree of integration between models, through the mediation of the data base system in which all deposit their outputs and from which they obtain their inputs.

The last dimension is integration in use rather than in the process. This is the degree to which the outputs of the different systems are complementary and join together to provide a coherent picture. Beyond compatibility in outputs, systems should aim for semantic integration at the level of the individual user, where, for each user, separate pieces of data blend into a single coordinated image of his area of interest.

To a large extent, the degree of integration reflects the other system characteristic, because it is dependent on the processing capabilities of the system, its data base, and its mode of operation. Similarly, it is dependent on the degree of sophistication, or maturity, of the organization with respect to information systems. The information system cannot be more highly integrated or sophisticated than the organization it serves. Thus the degree of integration is an expression of the interface between technological and organizational factors in the information system.

Individual Fit

The concept of individual fit arises from the perception that because people with different cognitive styles need different information, information systems should be adapted to their users. The importance of good fit between information systems and their users is clear—when the fit is bad, systems will not be used and so will be unsuccessful. Good individual fit is indispensable to use and success of MIS.

We will briefly recapitulate the discussion of users' styles in chapter 7 and then show by example how different system characteristics can interact with these styles.

Following Jung, the cognitive styles of individuals are composed of two independent functions—information input or perception, in which the individual senses objects in the world around him, and information analysis or evaluation, in which the individual considers the implications of his perceptions. Each function is performed in one of two dominant modes; the individual's cognitive style is a combination of a mode of perception and a mode of analysis.[17]

In the receptive mode of perception, attention is focused on isolated items of detailed factual data whereas in the preceptive mode, attention is focused on relationships between objects or stimuli, and situations are perceived in totality as gestalts. One mode of information evaluation utilizes formalistic methods of arrangement and analysis whereas the other mode is intuitive and heuristic. Each individual usually adopts one mode of perception and one mode of evaluation and represses alternative modes. Thus, there are four combinations of modes of perception and evaluation, or cognitive styles: preceptive-analytic, receptive-analytic, preceptive-heuristic, and receptive-heuristic.

Different functions and areas of management are best served by different cognitive styles, or perhaps people with different cognitive styles are drawn to different areas. Whatever the selection mechanism, all cognitive styles are found in each organization. The problem then is to structure the information system so that it can cater to all styles as required.

The importance of adapting MIS to users is exemplified by a case reported by Hammond.[18] A sophisticated MIS was built for the manager of a division in a large conglomerate. When the manager was promoted, he was succeeded by one of his subordinates who had accompanied the system from its inception, and he used it. But when a third manager, from outside the division, took over, the MIS fell into disuse. We can only conclude that there was some incompatibility between the new manager and the system.

A few examples of the ways in which system characteristics interact with cognitive styles of users will allow us to draw some conclusions about the structuring of systems. First consider interactive problem solving—a mode of operation—and its interplay with the dimensions of cognitive style. An analytic problem solver would tend to choose the model best suited to his problem and would then like to be led systematically through the operation of this model. He would then adopt the solution of the model as his decision. A more heuristic problem solver would typically have no clear preconception of the best model to use, and would probably prefer simulations to analytic models. He would like to try a number of models in quick succession, without being very thorough about any of them, to get a feel for the situation. On the basis of this feeling he would make a decision, factoring in his own intuitions in addition to the results of the various models; his decision would probably not conform exactly to any one of them. Systems that provide an interactive problem-solving capability should provide support for both these styles.

The types of models available are also important along the preceptive-receptive dimension. On one hand, simple and limited models fail to give a sufficient picture, even for the receptive style, because relevant data elements are not included. On the other hand, large, all-inclusive models overwhelm most managers' ability to understand the underlying assumptions—even if they are preceptive by nature. Thus various levels of models should exist, from comprehensive models covering numbers of divisions, products or markets, to more detailed models focusing on single plants, departments, or planning periods. In such a setting, the user can tailor the system to his specific needs and style.

With respect to the data characteristics, content, and accuracy, the receptive type would like his data to relate directly to the problem and to be as accurate as possible. He would probably be rather disturbed if any data item were missing or if he found any significant inaccuracies. The preceptive type, on the other hand, would be much less worried about inaccuracies but would like to receive both directly and indirectly related data to form a complete picture.

We would also expect a similar dichotomy over the level of aggregation, which is a processing capability. Though the receptive executive would prefer detailed data, his preceptive colleague would like a summary statement permitting him to see the gestalt rather than each of its individual components. The general conclusion should be clear by now. Systems should contain data in as detailed form as possible and should provide a variety of powerful and flexible processing tools to enable each user to obtain data at any level and in any combination preferred and to process them with any manipulator that he desires within a reasonable time.

Clearly there are economic constraints on such demands. It is impossible to maintain all data in atomic form, to process them instantaneously, and to provide all possible tools for manipulating them. There are also behavioral constraints. The ability to tailor a system from an amorphous collection of data and models requires a level of sophistication and self-confidence that many users lack. Thus the system should also provide structured solutions for those who prefer them. Because users also tend to be possessive about "their" data and the models they build for processing them, they do not readily pass on the expertise and tools they have developed—a contributing reason for the lack of use of systems built for one manager by others.

Ideally, then, an MIS should provide as broad a base of data, models, and prestructured solutions as is feasible. The user can then draw on any combination of these elements that suits his purposes. This is a radical departure from the currently dominant practice of providing a single structured solution.

Organizational Fit

The economic constraints on MIS structure mentioned above exemplify the topic of this section; not only should systems cater to individual users, but they should also be adapted to the organizations in which they are embedded. We refer to this adaptation between information systems and organizations as "organizational fit." It has several aspects: the feasibility of the MIS for the particular organization, the integration of the MIS with the organization, and the extent to which the MIS reflects the organization's *weltansicht* or world-view.

Feasibility

The feasibility of an MIS for a particular organization is a combination of the feasibilities in three different areas—technical feasibility, economic feasibility, and organizational feasibility. The technical aspect of feasibility deals with the availability of physical resources and technologies required by the system being contemplated. Especially when a very advanced system is being considered, the necessary hardware or software or "brainware" may not be available. For example, it is infeasible to build a system to transmit high volumes of data over a communications network if only low-speed lines are available. Theoretical solutions to problems exist in many areas, but current computing capacity and existing algorithms render it infeasible to solve very large problems; two examples are large integer programs and long-range weather forecasts.

Finally, it may also be infeasible to recruit large numbers of highly skilled programmers or analysts. A historical example of this is IBM's experience with the operating system for its 360 series of computers; development fell far behind schedule and only by a massive recruitment of programmers from all over the world was the project brought to completion. This kind of solution is neither feasible for most organizations nor desirable for any.

The economic component of feasibility is expressed in several areas. First, in parallel with the availability of technical resources, there is the question of availability of budgetary resources with which to procure machines, programs, and people. If the cash flow or investment capital do not permit the outlays required to develop the system, it must be considered infeasible. Second, if the technical and economic resources can be obtained, the question is whether the payoff justifies the outlay. The factors relevant to answering this question have been discussed in some detail in previous chapters. MIS profitability or rate of return on investment were suggested, in chapter 1, as indicators of success. These same criteria were considered as goals in chapter 3, which discussed the MIS target. Chapter 4, the MIS project, considered system costs, potential benefits, and the cost/benefit equation in their relationship to project development. Clearly, an MIS can be economically feasible only if it falls within the range of investments acceptable to the organization and is competitive with other investment alternatives.

The final aspect of MIS feasibility is organizational—the degree to which the organization is ready to accept and use the particular system being considered. This topic, discussed in chapter 2, relates to the fit between the structure of the system and the organization. It deals with the compatibility between the characteristics of the MIS and the size, structure, time frame, maturity, and psychological climate of the organization. Some organizational factors, such as size and psychological climate, can be benevolent or hostile to MIS in general, whereas others, such as organizational structure or time frame, will be favorable to some MIS structures and detrimental to others. Just as an MIS can succeed only if it is technically and economically feasible, so must the organizational factors also be favorable to ensure a high probability of success.

Integration with the Organization

It is possible to base MIS on packaged applications that are offered for use without reference to the personality of the organization. It is also possible to computerize existing procedures without changing them or the organization. In both cases, the information system does not become fully involved in the organization and remains somewhat peripheral to it. A third possibility is to adapt the structure of the MIS while inducing changes in the organization to support the information system; in these circumstances, the MIS becomes closely enmeshed with the organization. This is what we define as integration of the information system with the organization.

The integrative method of MIS development is recommended throughout this book. MIS objectives should be derived from and contribute to overall corporate objectives. Planning, design, and implementation of MIS should be an organizational effort in which management, users, and implementors all participate; it should not be the isolated effort of a peripheral group of experts. The planning phase of the project calls for an analysis of the organization, its internal boundaries, and the flow of information across those boundaries. The design phase requires that the structure of the organization, the relationships between its parts, and the information flows between them be considered and perhaps changed. Top management and users should become involved in the implementation process and the organizational changes it incurs. The involvement of management at all levels in the development of MIS leads to the MIS becoming closely involved in the functioning of the organization rather than operating as a service unit. The result is an MIS with a structure that reflects the overall corporate character and design and that has become an integral and essential part of the organization.

Weltansicht

The view of the world, or *weltansicht*, of the organization and the degree to which the MIS reflects it is the third and last aspect of the organizational fit of systems. Mitroff, Nelson, and Mason suggest that many organizations develop a "story" based on the history of the organization, its foundation, beginnings, growth, successes, and failures.[19] This history creates a view of the world as seen through the eyes of the organization and is specific to it. Mitroff and his colleagues constructed a "myth information system" built on this premise; in their system, information was provided in the context of the organizational myth. Their findings from experiments with this system indicate that information is more useful when it is tied to such a myth which is meaningful to the user and, especially, to the organization of which he is a part and in which the information is meant to be used.

The structure of the information should reflect this organizational view of the world. Information presented in the abstract will have less impact on decisions than contextually relevant information. It has even been stated that it is less important that models of organizational functions contain complete or correct representations of reality than that they mirror the organization's perception of the reality.[20] The organizational myth is expressed both in the data content of the information system and in the presentation of that information. The content should include those data which are important to building a picture of the world from the organization's view; for a company with antitrust problems, market share data may be oriented to an evaluation of its monopoly position, whereas for a small company, data may be oriented toward the profit potential of increasing the market share and slanted in both cases to support the company's position and goals.

The organizational myth should also determine the context within which the data are presented—for example, market penetration potential for the small company whose goal is expansion or least profitable areas of business for the antitrust violator forced into contraction. The more closely the structure of the information system reflects the world as it affects the organization the more useful and the more used it will be.

This chapter has pointed out that the process of information system development should be directed toward the construction of MIS structured in such a way as to fit the needs of individuals in the organization, and of the organization as a whole. The main points of this fit are summarized in table 9-1.

Conclusions

This section briefly summarizes the conclusions and morals to be drawn from the material contained in the book. These generalized themes occur and recur in different contexts and in a number of chapters throughout the text. They point to two widespread fallacies and three concepts.

The Fallacy of The Critical Variable

Scanning a selection of the suggested readings shows that the MIS literature is replete with attempts to specify the definitive critical variable, which, when properly handled, promises MIS success. In fact, most of the articles in the field pose long lists of such critical variables, including user involvement, top management support, priorities, formats, data bases, budgets, and user

Table 9-1
Summary of MIS Structural Variables

Variables	Conclusions
System characteristics	Processing capabilities: MIS should be equipped with flexible and readily available tools for manipulating data.
	Data characteristics: systems should provide users with data content, accuracy, recency, frequency and feedback time according to their requirements.
	Data base: increases the responsiveness of MIS to user's needs, facilitates data independence, and increases data integrity.
	A data base may sometimes be developed from existing files, but a fresh start is often required.
	Mode of operation: On-line real-time (OLRT) is the preferred mode for MIS.
	Input/output characteristics: the interface between the user and MIS should be as natural as possible, preferably in English of standard usage, embedded in a story, and in convenient formats.
	Integration: the degree to which the MIS represent the total organization. The integration of data, of models, of models with data base and integration in use is dependent on the degree of sophistication, or maturity, of the organization, and reflects other system characteristics.
Individual fit	System characteristics should facilitate the fit of the MIS to the individual users according to their cognitive styles and information needs. MIS should provide a broad base of data and the ability to arbitrarily combine data and models as well as prestructured solutions.
Organizational fit	Feasibility: MIS should be technically, economically, and organizationally feasible to the specific organization.
	Integration: MIS structure and the organization should be mutually adapted so that the MIS will reflect the corporate character and will become an integral part of a more mature organization.
	Weltansicht: The MIS should reflect the view of the world which is peculiar to the organization.

education. All these variables and many more are indeed important. They were all discussed in the preceding chapters and their effects on the success and failure of MIS were indicated. However, the success of MIS requires that *all* the variables should be within acceptable limits. While any one of them may lead to the failure of a system, no one of them can guarantee its success. Thus, the people responsible for building MIS need to keep in mind a long list of topics to ensure that the system will succeed.

The Concept of Formalization—A Critical Metavariable

Having just rejected the notion of a single critical variable and having indicated the need to keep a long list of variables under control, we now propose a critical metavariable, formalization. The only way that the multiple facets of MIS development can be controlled is by formalizing the process to prevent the oversights and ambiguities caused by informal decision making.

In this context, there are three rules of formalization. First, all the decisions made with respect to the system and its development process should be conscious and explicit and cover all the relevant variables. Second, clear responsibility should be assigned for making, executing, and controlling such decisions. When decisions are made at the wrong level or when the execution of decisions is not controlled, failure often follows. Third, the entire development process, from strategic decisions, targets, and general approaches to technical execution at the programming and operations level, should be thoroughly documented. Documentation ensures that all decisions are made formally and that the precise intention of the decision can be recalled if necessary. Furthermore, documentation provides continuity in an environment usually characterized by high rates of technological change and of personnel turnover.

The Concept of Responsibility Assignment

The structure of this book roughly parallels the assignment of responsibility for the MIS development process. The process-oriented chapters are chapter 2, The MIS Environment; chapter 3, The MIS Target; and chapter 4, The MIS Project. The environmental assessment and higher level stages of target definition are the responsibility of top executives, discussed in chapter 5, Executive Responsibility. Chapter 7, Users of MIS, deals with the responsibility of users in helping to bridge the gap between general goals and specific systems; this role is expressed in the more detailed stages of target definition and in the higher level stages of the MIS project that evolves from the definition. The final stages of project development and operation are primarily the responsibility of MIS management and staff as discussed in chapter 6, Implementors of MIS. Although responsibilities do overlap, and the boundaries of jurisdictions vary from one organization to another, it is useful to remember the overall picture as a guide. It can help to prevent cases of incorrect or nonassignment of responsibilities.

The Fallacy of the Universal Solution

MIS are interwoven with many areas and activities in organizations. To assume that there is one best way to design and implement MIS is to assume that all organizations have the same characteristics and comply to some universal form. Clearly, neither assumption is true; one of our major themes is that each organization, its managers, and its MIS must undergo a process of mutual adjustment and adaptation. The end product of this process is a combination of an organization, its managers, and their information systems that is unique to that organization and can rarely be emulated by any other. Because the factors requiring mutual adjustment and their nature vary from one organization to another it is incorrect to propose a universal plan or solution for MIS development

The Concept of Contingency Planning

Because no universal plan is possible for MIS development, the concept of contingency planning is the natural alternative. In the context of MIS, this concept states that a large number of variables have to be considered and decisions made about each one. Each combination of variables is unique to each organization and no general statement can be made about the correct decision for each such unique set of values in its entirety. We can look at closely related groups of variables and decide what should be done in each situation, or contingency, relating to such a group. The absence of any universal scheme places a heavy responsibility on managers at all levels to understand the specific situation of their particular organization and how best to handle it. One cannot buy MIS off the shelf—they must be tailored to each organization.

Notes

1. R.O. Mason and I.I. Mitroff, "A Program for Research on Management Information Systems," *Management Science*, vol. 19, no. 5 (January 1973), pp. 475-487.

2. Theodore F. Mock, "A Longitudinal Study of Some Information Structure Alternatives," *Data Base*, vol. 5, nos. 2, 3, and 4 (Winter 1973), pp. 40-49.

3. J.D. Aron, "Information Systems in Perspective," *Computing Surveys*, vol. 1, no. 4 (December 1969), pp. 213-236.

4. Henry Mintzberg, "Making Management Information Useful," *Management Review*, vol. 64, no. 5 (May 1975), pp. 34-38.

5. Norman L. Chervany and Gary W. Dickson, "An Experimental Evaluation of Information Overload in a Production Environment," *Management Science*, vol. 20, no. 10 (June 1974), pp. 1335-44.

6. R.A. Kronenberg, "Weyerhaeuser's Management Information System," *Datamation*, vol. 13, no. 5 (May 1967), pp. 28-30.

7. See, for example, Ian I. Mitroff, John Nelson, and Richard O. Mason, "On Management Myth-Information Systems," *Management Science*, vol. 21, no. 4 (December 1974), pp. 371-382; Henry Mintzberg, "The Myths of MIS," *California Management Review*, vol. XV, no. 1 (Fall 1972), pp. 92-97; and Mintzberg, "Making Management Information Useful."

8. See, for example, Kent W. Colton, "Computers and Police: Patterns of Success and Failure," *Sloan Management Review*, vol. 14, no. 2 (Winter 1972-73), pp. 75-97; Henry C. Lucas, Jr., "A Descriptive Model of Information Systems in the Context of the Organization, *Data Base*, vol. 5, nos. 2, 3, and 4 (Winter 1973), pp. 27-39; and Mock, "A Longitudinal Study of Some Information Structure Alternatives."

9. Charles H. Kriebel, "The Future MIS," *Business Automation*, vol. 19, no. 6 (June 1972), pp. 18 ff.

10. Richard L. Nolan, "Computer Data Base: The Future is Now," *Harvard Business Review*, vol. 51, no. 5 (September-October 1973), pp. 98-114.

11. Good examples are C. Date, *An Introduction to Database Systems* (Reading, Mass.: Addison-Wesley, 1975), and James Thomas Martin, *Computer Data-Base Organization* (Englewood Cliffs, N.J.: Prentice-Hall, 1975).

12. H. Sackman, "Experimental Analysis of Human Behavior in Time Sharing and Batch Processing Information Systems" in *Management Information Systems: Progress and Perspectives*, ed. C.K. Kriebel, R.L. Van Horn, and T.J. Heames (Pittsburgh: Carnegie Press, 1971). See also Ronald A. Seaberg and Charlotte Seaberg, "Computer-Based Decision Systems in Xerox Corporate Planning," *Management Science,* vol. 20, no. 4, Part 2 (December 1973), pp. 575-584.

13. Robert V. Head, "The Elusive MIS," *Datamation*, vol. 16, no. 10 (September 1970), pp. 22-27.

14. I.K. Cohen and Richard L. Van Horn, "A Laboratory Research Approach to Organizational Design," European Institute for Advanced Studies in Management, Working Paper 72-16 (April 1972).

15. Ian I. Mitroff, John Nelson, and Richard O. Mason, "On Management Myth-Information Systems," *Management Science*, vol. 21, no. 4 (December 1974), pp. 371-382.

16. Robert B. Ochsman and Alphonse Chapanis, "The Effects of 10 Communication Modes on the Behavior of Teams during Co-operative

Problem-Solving," *International Journal of Man-Machine Studies*, vol. 6, no. 5 (1974), pp. 579-619.

17. James L. McKenney and Peter G.W. Keen, "How Managers' Minds Work." *Harvard Business Review*, vol. 25, no. 3 (May-June 1973), pp. 131-142. See also Mason and Mitroff, "A Program for Research on Management Information Systems."

18. John S. Hammond III, "Do's and Don't's of Computer Models for Planning," *Harvard Business Review*, vol. 52, no. 2 (March-April 1974), pp. 110-123.

19. Mitroff, Nelson and Mason, "On Management Myth-Information Systems."

20. Robert H. Hayes and Richard L. Nolan, "What Kind of Corporate Modeling Functions Best," *Harvard Business Review*, vol. 52, no. 3 (May-June 1974), pp. 102-112.

Suggested Readings

Mason, R.O. and Mitroff, I.I. "A Program for Research on Management Information Systems." *Management Science*, vol. 19, no. 5 (January 1973), pp. 475-487.

Mintzberg, Henry. "Making Management Information Useful." *Management Review*, vol. 64, no. 5 (May 1975), pp. 34-38.

Mitroff, Ian I., Nelson, John, and Mason, Richard O. "On Management Myth-Information Systems." *Management Science*, vol. 21, no. 4 (December 1974), pp. 371-382.

Nolan, Richard L. "Computer Data Base: The Future is Now." *Harvard Business Review*, vol. 51, no. 5 (September-October 1973), pp. 98-114.

Sackman, H. "Experimental Analysis of Human Behavior in Time Sharing and Batch Processing Information Systems" in Kriebel, C.K., Van Horn, R.L., and Heames, T.J. (eds.) *Management Information Systems: Progress and Perspectives*. Pittsburgh: Carnegie Press, 1971.

Seaberg, Ronald A. and Seaberg, Charlotte. "Computer-Based Decision Systems in Xerox Corporate Planning." *Management Science*, vol. 20, no.4, Part 2 (December 1973), pp. 575-584.

Index

Index

abandonment evaluation, 75-76
accounting, 36, 84; firms, 92
accuracy, 62, 70, 78, 164, 172
Ackoff, Russel L., 133
aerospace, 27, 89
aggregation, level of, 47, 52, 139, 163, 173
agriculture, 51
airlines, 34, 51, 168
airport, 37
algorithm, 38, 174
American Airlines, 83
analysis, mode of, 171
analysts, 30, 31, 174; career paths, 126; study and design, 73-75
analytical tools, 53
Anthony, Robert N., 3, 5, 7, 12
applications, 19, 48, 56; packages, 82, 83, 175
Argyris, Chris, 144, 152, 157
Arkwright—Boston Manufacturers Mutual Insurance Company, 102
Association for Computing Machinery (ACM), 113
association with MIS, 99; perception of, 105
asymmetry of relations, top management-user, 149-150
ATPP, 122
attitudes, 31, 33, 34, 68, 78, 109, 169; organizational, 89; prior, 141-143
Avis, 152

bank, 2, 5, 7, 8, 62, 151, 168
basic chemicals, 28
batch processing, 70, 168
benefits, 8, 59, 61, 62; intangible, 33, 61; tangible, 33, 61
bottom-up. See directions of attack
Brady, Rodney H., 135
budget: allocations, 30, 89; goals, 61; planning and control systems, 62; specifications, 71; supplementary, 71
Bureau of Labor Statistics, 119

capabilities, 113; analysts, 119-120; implementors, 115-116; programmers, 119-120; supervisors, 116-118
capital budgeting, 59
career paths, 113, 121; programmers, 125-126; supervisors, 126-127
cash flow, 24, 53, 58, 174
centralization, 24, 48, 85, 86, 87, 90, 92; advantages, 86; computer resource, 25; data base, 25; disadvantages, 86; hardware, 81, 85; MIS development, 25; MIS unit, 25, 85-87; organization, 25, 50; resources, 92
Certificate in Data Processing, 113
change resistance, 131, 145, 153, 157
cognitive styles, 152, 153, 156, 163, 171, 172
commercial aircraft industry, 26
communications, 86, 154, 158; mode of, 170; networks, 39, 174; systems, 38, 51; top management-implementor, 151-152; top management-user, 149, 151; user-implementor, 152-153
computer. See hardware
Computer Programmer Aptitude Battery, 122
conflict, 124, 144, 155; user-implementor, 154-156
conflict reduction; user-implementor, 154-156
consultants, 83, 92, 93, 103
consulting: firms, 122; services, 92-93
contingency planning, concept of, 179
control, 62; controller, 102; cycles, 151; function, 15, 63; hierarchy, 5, 21; managerial, 68; operations, 106; processes, 28; project, 68-69, top management-implementors, 151
cooperation, 117; user-implementor, 156-157
corporate: character, 175; computer staff, 83, 89-90; levels, 101; models, 104; personality, 50; planning and control, 61, 102

185

About the Authors

Phillip Ein-Dor is a senior lecturer in the Faculty of Management, Tel-Aviv University, Tel-Aviv, Israel. He received the Ph.D. and M.Sc. from Carnegie-Mellon University, and the B.A. from Hebrew University of Jerusalem. He has published a number of articles in scientific and professional journals on various aspects of computers and information system management. In addition to his academic work, he is also active as a consultant in this field to a number of public and private organizations.

Eli Segev is a senior lecturer in the Faculty of Management, Tel-Aviv University. He received the D.B.A. from Harvard Business School, M.B.A. from Tel-Aviv University, and B.Sc. from Technion, Israel Institute of Technology. He has published a number of articles on strategic decision making, management use of information, and management information systems in *Management Science, Academy of Management Review, MSU Business Topics, Journal of Management Studies*, and other leading American and European management journals.